SMYTHE LIBRARY

Stamp this label with the date for return.
Contact the Librarian if you wish to renew this book.

D0229548

H72832J0502

GREAT SPEECHES
OF THE
20TH CENTURY

GREAT SPEECHES
OF THE
20TH CENTURY

Emmeline Pankhurst · Virginia Woolf
Franklin D Roosevelt · Winston Churchill
Charles de Gaulle · Jawaharlal Nehru
Nikita Khrushchev · Aneurin Bevan
Harold Macmillan · John F Kennedy
Martin Luther King · Nelson Mandela
Margaret Thatcher · Earl Spencer

Edited by Tom Clark

preface
theguardian

Published by Preface 2008

10 9 8 7 6 5 4 3 2

This book is sold subject to the condition that it shall not, by way
of trade or otherwise, be lent, resold, hired out, or otherwise circulated without
the publisher's prior consent in any form of binding or cover other than that
in which it is published and without a similar condition, including this
condition, being imposed on the subsequent purchaser

First published in Great Britain in 2008 by
Preface Publishing
Random House, 20 Vauxhall Bridge Road,
London SW1V 2SA

www.randomhouse.co.uk
www.rbooks.co.uk
www.prefacepublishing.co.uk

Addresses for companies within The Random House Group Limited
can be found at: www.randomhouse.co.uk

The Random House Group Limited Reg. No. 954009

A CIP catalogue record for this book is available from the British Library

ISBN 9781848090385

Every effort has been made to contact copyright holders. However,
the publishers will be glad to rectify in future editions any inadvertent
omissions brought to their attention.

The Random House Group Limited supports the Forest Stewardship
Council® (FSC®), the leading international forest-certification organisation. Our books
carrying the FSC label are printed on FSC®-certified paper. FSC is the only forest-certification
scheme supported by the leading environmental organisations, including Greenpeace.
Our paper procurement policy can be found at www.randomhouse.co.uk/environment

Typeset in 10.75 on 15pt Adobe Caslon
by Palimpsest Book Production Limited,
Grangemouth, Stirlingshire
Printed and bound in Great Britain by
MPG Printgroup

909.82 CLA
R728325

MIX
Paper from
responsible sources
FSC   FSC® C018575
www.fsc.org

CONTENTS

CONTENTS

Introduction

Tom Clark, Editor

The man who first spelled out the ground rules for great speeches was himself blessed with the sharpest tongue in Rome. Cicero used it to attain high office, win court cases and secure changes to the policy of the Roman Republic.

It could not, however, protect him from the broader sweep of history. As the Republic began to give way to the Empire, Cicero was decapitated.

Fulvia, the wife of Mark Antony, is said to have pulled out the famously fluent tongue from his severed head and jabbed it with her hairpin.

Great oratory can send a shiver down the spine, but a speech will only be truly great when it chimes with the times in which it is delivered. That is what unifies this collection of *Great Speeches of the 20th Century* – it is what enabled them to change the world.

Several of the speeches established in the public mind a personality of great importance. For example, Charles de Gaulle's wartime broadcasts began his journey to being regarded as the saviour of France. Likewise, the towering personality of 1980s Britain was only established once Margaret Thatcher stood up and insisted that despite rocketing unemployment 'the lady's not for turning'.

In another of the speeches, made by Nikita Khrushchev to the Soviet Union's Communist party in 1956, this process is reversed. An even more important personality – that of Stalin – was decisively demolished.

Other speeches again rally opponents of the powerful, by welding arguments together into a devastating weapon. In very different ways, this was achieved both by Nelson Mandela's speech from the dock in his 1964 treason trial and Aneurin Bevan's masterly parliamentary demolition job on the Eden government's case for making war on Egypt in 1956.

In a different age Earl Spencer's eulogy to his sister, Princess Diana, delicately but unsparingly condemning the cruelty of the media and the coldness of the royal family, had a similar effect.

Many great speeches paint a picture of what a better world might be like.

But for some – most obviously Martin Luther King's 'I have a dream' – the transmission of this vision around the world was itself a significant political consequence.

Though their consequences are varied, each of the speeches in this selection had an impact on the world. The same reasoning explains many omissions from the collection. In his mastery of the rhetorical art alone, Margaret Thatcher's Labour opponent Neil Kinnock frequently outdid her. It is history – a history that put her in power, and him in opposition – that ensures it is her speeches that are now remembered.

Influential speeches are given by those to whom society is ready to listen.

Often this rules out many people. For much of the 20th century, women struggled to make themselves heard, and that is the principal reason for the depressing male domination of the collection.

Indeed, the two female contributors that we do have from the century's early years – Emmeline Pankhurst in her 1913 American lecture on the war being waged by the suffragettes, and Virginia Woolf, speaking at the Cambridge lectures that were to become *A Room of One's Own* – both shed valuable light on how female voices were drowned out.

If historical circumstance is the most important factor in any great speech, the choice of the right words for the occasion is another essential part of the mix.

It was the former governor of New York, Mario Cuomo, who said: 'You campaign in poetry, but you must govern in prose'.

In a parliamentary setting an effective speech deploys forensic rigour enlivened with wit. But a great performance at a political rally is very different – more than anything, it requires emotive language to provoke the right mix of inspiration and indignation.

But even where great speeches have very different form and purpose, there are some rhetorical ingredients – like good cooking oil in the kitchen – that come in useful with all sorts of dishes. There are tricks of the trade, many known to orators since Cicero's time, that crop up time and again.

One of the most basic is the 'rule of three'. No one quite knows why, but speakers have always found that by clumping things together in threes they can hammer home their message.

De Gaulle put the rule to particularly good use. Instead of calling on men who have served in 'any of France's armed forces' he issued his summons in sequence to men of the army, navy and air forces ('de terre, de mer et de l'air'). The rhythm reinforces the entreaty for everyone to do their bit.

After a decade of New Labour, many are disdainful of soundbites, but turning a phrase that encapsulates a message has always been an essential part of crafting a great speech, and it remains so.

Even the best soundbites rely on very old tricks. One is phrase reversal – John F Kennedy's 'ask not what your country can do for you, but what you can do for your country'. Another is taking an established cliché and adapting it. Margaret Thatcher, for example, wheeled out the then well-worn phrase about Labour's 'winter of discontent' but then held out promise in its place of 'an autumn of understanding' and 'a winter of common sense'.

One of the oldest oratorical controversies was whether, however artful the craftsmanship, a great speech must in the end be animated by the veracity of its argument. Even before Cicero, Plato insisted against the Sophists that it must be – 2,500 years later the dispute remains a live one.

We ran into it considering Enoch Powell's anti-immigration 'rivers of blood' speech, made in 1968 as Kenyan Asians arrived in the UK. Powell was a classical scholar, steeped in the rhetoric of the ancient world, and he drew on it heavily – even, in line with the best Roman practice, enhancing the urgency of his tone by holding in his urine in advance of delivering a big speech.

His speeches were said to 'smell of the wick' – he sat late into the night, weaving in allusions to and oratorical tricks from the ancient world. Much of that is in 'rivers of blood', and no doubt it helped create the immediate impact, seen as racist protesters came out onto the streets in support of a man who they felt had finally articulated their fears.

Looking back at the text today, well-crafted as the words are, they look pernicious above all else. More than that, the predictions they make have proved unambiguously false – immigration happened, and the blood was not spilt in the way Powell predicted. In the end, although remarkable, Powell's notorious speech falls short of being great.

As the 20th century wore on, what audiences expected changed, and great speech-makers had to adapt. Public meetings ceased to be the draw that they once were, and – in an increasingly distracting world – attention spans declined. No modern political leader would write a speech running to tens of thousands of words, as Pankhurst and Khrushchev did, when it would mean expecting audiences to sit still and listen for hours at a time. We had to edit down several speeches, and especially those from the century's early years.

Another huge change was technological. A momentous speech would traditionally reach most people as newsprint; but as first radio and then TV became all-important that changed. Delivery came to matter to those beyond the immediate audience, and truly great delivery – like that of Martin Luther King, who harnessed his voice as a virtuoso would a Stradivarius – developed an enhanced capacity to propel speeches into greatness.

So some of the criteria of greatness have evolved. But looking across a series that stretches from 1913 to 1997, what is equally striking is one constant: namely, the extraordinary and enduring power of the spoken word.

Freedom or death

Emmeline Pankhurst
November 13 1913

This is an edited version of a speech delivered by
Emmeline Pankhurst in Hartford, Connecticut,
on November 13 1913.

For ease of reading, individual excisions are not marked,
nor is it indicated when the case of a letter changes
due to the deletion of part of a sentence.

Germaine Greer

Germaine Greer is a writer, academic and feminist.

Emmeline Pankhurst made her most famous speech on a fundraising tour of the US in autumn 1913. During the preceding 18 months she had been imprisoned 12 times, but had served no more than 30 days, all of them on hunger strike. According to her daughter and comrade, Christabel Pankhurst, prison staff never dared to force-feed her. In response to public revulsion, force-feeding was abandoned in 1913 and the 'Cat and Mouse Act' brought in, which provided that fasting female inmates whose health was suffering be released until their health improved, then re-arrested as often as necessary until their sentence was served out. As Pankhurst informed one American audience: 'They sent me to prison, to penal servitude for three years. I came out of prison at the end of nine days. I broke my prison bars. Four times they took me back again; four times I burst the prison door open again. And I left England openly to come and visit America, with only three or four weeks of the three years' sentence of penal servitude served. Have we not proved, then, that they cannot govern human beings who withhold their consent?'

Between spells in prison Pankhurst several times addressed audiences from a stretcher. Few people were photographed more often or to better effect. She even managed to be photographed in prison garb. From 1909 to 1914 untold numbers of badges bearing her photograph were sold for a penny each. Her speeches are those of a media celebrity, who knows that her audience is first of all curious to see her, regardless of whether they agree with her or not.

Rebecca West recalled hearing her lecture: 'Trembling like a reed, she lifted up her hoarse, sweet voice on the platform, but the reed was of steel and it was tremendous.' Small, very slim, and usually fashionably gowned and hatted, Pankhurst projected a conscientiously feminine image. The American popular press, even as it sneered at the cause of women's suffrage, agreed that she was a great entertainer. She delivered her 'freedom or death' speech at Hartford, Connecticut, on November 13 1913, before an audience assembled by the Connecticut Women's Suffrage Association, under the leadership of Katherine Houghton Hepburn (mother of the film star). Pankhurst's audience was aware that, five months earlier, on June 4 1913, the Women's Social and Political Union (WSPU) member Emily Davison had run on to the track in front of the King's horse when it was running in the Derby. The horse cannoned into her, somersaulted, and the jockey was thrown badly. Davison never regained consciousness and died four days later. The well-known fact remains unspoken in Pankhurst's speech, which hardly makes sense without it. Both she and Christabel accepted Davison's act as deliberate martyrdom and defied timid spirits who doubted Davison was sane.

Pankhurst's task was to use her lecture to justify the adoption by the WSPU of such militant tactics. 'Deeds not Words', as their slogan and Emily Davison's tombstone had it, had alienated the greater part of the British suffragist movement. Pankhurst begins by inviting her audience to consider the absurdity of treating someone such as her as a dangerous criminal. She then reminds her Yankee audience of their own tradition of revolution and civil war, subtly persuading them that not to allow women to use violence, when they had fought two wars to free themselves and to end slavery, was inconsistent. Then, startlingly, she attacks the very sympathy that has welcomed her to Hartford. She tells her audience that she doesn't care if she alienates sympathisers, because suffragists in England had enjoyed public sympathy for 50 years and it never brought them anything. Destructiveness, including self-destructiveness, was the only way.

The British government was well aware of the high profile of the WSPU and Emmeline Pankhurst. Within days of the declaration of war against Germany on August 4 1914, the government was negotiating for WSPU assistance in drumming up support for the war. On August 10, the government agreed to release all WSPU prisoners and paid the WSPU £2,000 to organise a patriotic rally, which was attended by 30,000 people. Under the slogan 'Men must fight and women must work,' Pankhurst exhorted the trades unions to allow women to work in jobs traditionally done by men. In 1918, women got the vote – or rather, women over 30, who were householders, wives of householders or landholders, got the vote. Pankhurst's civil war ended, as all wars must, in negotiation.

Freedom or death

EMMELINE PANKHURST
November 13 1913

I do not come here as an advocate, because whatever position
the suffrage movement may occupy in the United States of
America, in England it has passed beyond the realm of advo-
cacy and it has entered into the sphere of practical politics. It
has become the subject of revolution and civil war, and so
tonight I am not here to advocate woman suffrage. American
suffragists can do that very well for themselves.

I am here as a soldier who has temporarily left the field
of battle in order to explain – it seems strange it should
have to be explained – what civil war is like when civil war
is waged by women. I am not only here as a soldier
temporarily absent from the field of battle; I am here – and
that, I think, is the strangest part of my coming – I am here
as a person who, according to the law courts of my country,
it has been decided, is of no value to the community at all;
and I am adjudged because of my life to be a dangerous
person, under sentence of penal servitude in a convict prison.

It is not at all difficult if revolutionaries come to you from Russia, if they come to you from China, or from any other part of the world, if they are men. But since I am a woman it is necessary to explain why women have adopted revolutionary methods in order to win the rights of citizenship. We women, in trying to make our case clear, always have to make as part of our argument, and urge upon men in our audience the fact – a very simple fact – that women are human beings.

Suppose the men of Hartford had a grievance, and they laid that grievance before their legislature, and the legislature obstinately refused to listen to them, or to remove their grievance, what would be the proper and the constitutional and the practical way of getting their grievance removed? Well, it is perfectly obvious at the next general election the men of Hartford would turn out that legislature and elect a new one.

But let the men of Hartford imagine that they were not in the position of being voters at all, that they were governed without their consent being obtained, that the legislature turned an absolutely deaf ear to their demands, what would the men of Hartford do then? They couldn't vote the legislature out. They would have to choose; they would have to make a choice of two evils: they would either have to submit indefinitely to an unjust state of affairs, or they would have to rise up and adopt some of the antiquated means by which men in the past got their grievances remedied.

Your forefathers decided that they must have representation

for taxation, many, many years ago. When they felt they couldn't wait any longer, when they laid all the arguments before an obstinate British government that they could think of, and when their arguments were absolutely disregarded, when every other means had failed, they began by the tea party at Boston, and they went on until they had won the independence of the United States of America.

It is about eight years since the word militant was first used to describe what we were doing. It was not militant at all, except that it provoked militancy on the part of those who were opposed to it. When women asked questions in political meetings and failed to get answers, they were not doing anything militant. In Great Britain it is a custom, a time-honoured one, to ask questions of candidates for parliament and ask questions of members of the government. No man was ever put out of a public meeting for asking a question. The first people who were put out of a political meeting for asking questions, were women; they were brutally ill-used; they found themselves in jail before 24 hours had expired.

We were called militant, and we were quite willing to accept the name. We were determined to press this question of the enfranchisement of women to the point where we were no longer to be ignored by the politicians.

You have two babies very hungry and wanting to be fed. One baby is a patient baby, and waits indefinitely until its mother is ready to feed it. The other baby is an impatient baby and cries lustily, screams and kicks and makes

9

everybody unpleasant until it is fed. Well, we know perfectly well which baby is attended to first. That is the whole history of politics. You have to make more noise than anybody else, you have to make yourself more obtrusive than anybody else, you have to fill all the papers more than anybody else, in fact you have to be there all the time and see that they do not snow you under.

When you have warfare things happen; people suffer; the noncombatants suffer as well as the combatants. And so it happens in civil war. When your forefathers threw the tea into Boston Harbour, a good many women had to go without their tea. It has always seemed to me an extra-ordinary thing that you did not follow it up by throwing the whiskey overboard; you sacrificed the women; and there is a good deal of warfare for which men take a great deal of glorification which has involved more practical sacrifice on women than it has on any man. It always has been so. The grievances of those who have got power, the influence of those who have got power commands a great deal of attention; but the wrongs and the grievances of those people who have no power at all are apt to be absolutely ignored. That is the history of humanity right from the beginning.

Well, in our civil war people have suffered, but you cannot make omelettes without breaking eggs; you cannot have civil war without damage to something. The great thing is to see that no more damage is done than is absolutely necessary, that you do just as much as will arouse enough feeling to bring about peace, to bring about an honorable peace for the combatants; and that is what we have been doing.

We entirely prevented stockbrokers in London from telegraphing to stockbrokers in Glasgow and vice versa: for one whole day telegraphic communication was entirely stopped. I am not going to tell you how it was done. I am not going to tell you how the women got to the mains and cut the wires; but it was done. It was done, and it was proved to the authorities that weak women, suffrage women, as we are supposed to be, had enough ingenuity to create a situation of that kind. Now, I ask you, if women can do that, is there any limit to what we can do except the limit we put upon ourselves?

If you are dealing with an industrial revolution, if you get the men and women of one class rising up against the men and women of another class, you can locate the difficulty; if there is a great industrial strike, you know exactly where the violence is and how the warfare is going to be waged; but in our war against the government you can't locate it. We wear no mark; we belong to every class; we permeate every class of the community from the highest to the lowest; and so you see in the woman's civil war the dear men of my country are discovering it is absolutely impossible to deal with it: you cannot locate it, and you cannot stop it.

'Put them in prison,' they said; 'that will stop it.' But it didn't stop it at all: instead of the women giving it up, more women did it, and more and more and more women did it until there were 300 women at a time, who had not broken a single law, only 'made a nuisance of themselves' as the politicians say.

Then they began to legislate. The British government has passed more stringent laws to deal with this agitation than it ever found necessary during all the history of political agitation in my country. They were able to deal with the revolutionaries of the Chartists' time: they were able to deal with the trades union agitation; they were able to deal with the revolutionaries later on when the Reform Acts were passed: but the ordinary law has not sufficed to curb insurgent women. They had to dip back into the middle ages to find a means of repressing the women in revolt.

They have said to us, government rests upon force, the women haven't force, so they must submit. Well, we are showing them that government does not rest upon force at all: it rests upon consent.

As long as women consent to be unjustly governed, they can be, but directly women say: 'We withhold our consent, we will not be governed any longer so long as that government is unjust.' Not by the forces of civil war can you govern the very weakest woman. You can kill that woman, but she escapes you then; you cannot govern her. No power on earth can govern a human being, however feeble, who withholds his or her consent.

When they put us in prison at first, simply for taking petitions, we submitted; we allowed them to dress us in prison clothes; we allowed them to put us in solitary confinement; we allowed them to put us amongst the most degraded of criminals; we learned of some of the appalling evils of our so-called civilisation that we could not have learned in any other way. It was valuable experience, and we were glad to get it.

I have seen men smile when they heard the words 'hunger strike', and yet I think there are very few men today who would be prepared to adopt a 'hunger strike' for any cause. It is only people who feel an intolerable sense of oppression who would adopt a means of that kind. It means, you refuse food until you are at death's door, and then the authorities have to choose between letting you die, and letting you go; and then they let the women go.

Now, that went on so long that the government felt that they were unable to cope. It was [then] that, to the shame of the British government, they set the example to authorities all over the world of feeding sane, resisting human beings by force. There may be doctors in this meeting: if so, they know it is one thing to feed by force an insane person; but it is quite another thing to feed a sane, resisting human being who resists with every nerve and with every fibre of her body the indignity and the outrage of forcible feeding.

Now, that was done in England, and the government thought they had crushed us. But they found that it did not quell the agitation, that more and more women came in and even passed that terrible ordeal, and they were obliged to let them go.

Then came the legislation the 'Cat and Mouse Act'. The

home secretary said, 'give me the power to let these women go when they are at death's door, and leave them at liberty under license until they have recovered their health again and then bring them back.' It was passed to repress the agitation, to make the women yield – because that is what it has really come to, ladies and gentlemen. It has come to a battle between the women and the government as to who shall yield first, whether they will yield and give us the vote, or whether we will give up our agitation.

Well, they little know what women are. Women are very slow to rouse, but once they are aroused, once they are determined, nothing on earth and nothing in heaven will make women give way; it is impossible. And so this 'Cat and Mouse Act' which is being used against women today has failed. There are women lying at death's door, recovering enough strength to undergo operations who have not given in and won't give in, and who will be prepared, as soon as they get up from their sick beds, to go on as before. There are women who are being carried from their sick beds on stretchers into meetings. They are too weak to speak, but they go amongst their fellow workers just to show that their spirits are unquenched, and that their spirit is alive, and they mean to go on as long as life lasts.

Now, I want to say to you who think women cannot succeed, we have brought the government of England to this position, that it has to face this alternative: either women are to be killed or women are to have the vote. I ask American men in this meeting, what would you say if in your state you were faced with that alternative, that you must either kill them or give them their citizenship? Well, there is only one answer to that alternative, there is only one way out, you must give those women the vote.

You won your freedom in America when you had the revolution, by bloodshed, by sacrificing human life. You won the civil war by the sacrifice of human life when you decided to emancipate the negro. You have left it to women in your land, the men of all civilised countries have left it to women, to work out their own salvation. That is the way in which we women of England are doing. Human life for us is sacred, but we say if any life is to be sacrificed it shall be ours; we won't do it ourselves, but we will put the enemy in the position where they will have to choose between giving us freedom or giving us death.

So here am I. I come in the intervals of prison appearance. I come after having been four times imprisoned under the 'Cat and Mouse Act', probably going back to be rearrested as soon as I set my foot on British soil. I come to ask you to help to win this fight. If we win it, this hardest of all fights, then, to be sure, in the future it is going to be made easier for women all over the world to win their fight when their time comes.

The Connecticut speech was not reported in the
Manchester Guardian, but this story, covering Emmeline
Pankhurst's arrest a short time before, reports her
rehearsing similar arguments. It ran on February 25 1913.

MRS PANKHURST ARRESTED
Charge of inciting to the bomb outrage

Mrs Pankhurst, the leader of the Women's Social and Political
Union, was arrested in London yesterday. In effect, she is
charged with having 'feloniously counselled and procured
certain persons whose names are unknown' to commit the
bomb outrage last week at Mr Lloyd George's unoccupied
house. Mrs Pankhurst was in custody at Leatherhead police
station last night, and will be brought before the magistrate
at Epsom this morning.

The Home Office authorities have for some days had
under consideration the speech delivered by Mrs Pankhurst
at Cardiff on Wednesday, the night following the bomb
outrage. In this speech Mrs Pankhurst recalled that, when
the Franchise Bill was withdrawn, 'I told them that I was
prepared to accept responsibility for all acts to which women
felt themselves driven.' She is reported as saying: 'I have
incited; I have conspired; and I say this – that the authorities need not look for the women who have done what they

did last night. I accept responsibility for it. If tomorrow I am arrested for what happened and sent to penal servitude, I shall prove in my own person that the punishment cannot be carried out. If they send me for 5 years, 10 years, or 20 years, I shall not stay. I shall at once hunger strike. If they torture me with force-feeding, that cannot last very long; they cannot keep me alive very long; and they will have to let me die or let me go. If I drop out of the fight hundreds will take my place.'

Effect on the militants

The meeting of the militant Union at the London Pavilion yesterday afternoon was made a very noisy one by the interruptions and shouting of men. The speakers declared emphatically that militancy would go on, and that Mrs Pankhurst's arrest would strengthen their movement.

After the window-smashing campaign of last March, Mrs Pankhurst and Mr and Mrs Pethwick Lawrence (then associated as officers of the Women's Social and Political Union) were proceeded against for conspiracy, and on May 22 were each sentenced at the Old Bailey to nine months imprisonment.

They were transferred to the first division, but eventually joined in a hunger strike as a protest against the withholding of similar treatment from other suffragist prisoners. Mrs Pankhurst and Mrs Pethwick Lawrence were released on June 24 owing to the state of their health, and Mr Pethwick Lawrence was liberated a few days later.

The warrant and the arrest

The warrant charges Mrs Pankhurst with 'having on the 19th day of February, 1913, feloniously, unlawfully, and maliciously counselled and procured persons whose names are unknown to feloniously, unlawfully, and maliciously place in a certain building gunpowder and explosive substances with intent thereby to damage the said building, contrary to the Malicious Injury to Property Act 1861.'

Seen last night at the police station, Mrs Pankhurst told a press representative that she was receiving every reasonable consideration from the police, being allowed to select her own food and have writing materials. It was probable that she would not open her defence today, as she would be remanded for perhaps a week or more. Asked if she had expected arrest, Mrs Pankhurst smilingly replied: 'You know that I was engaged to speak at the Pavilion this afternoon, when I might have had something startling to say, but that will keep now until trial.'

Mrs Pankhurst went on to deprecate the unjust course it seemed to her so many people were taking in ignoring the fact that women are a disenfranchised class without the ordinary constitutional means of pressure upon Parliament. 'We shall fight against the condition of affairs,' she said, 'so long as life is in us.'

Shakespeare's sister

VIRGINIA WOOLF
October 20 and 26 1928

Versions of this speech were delivered by Virginia Woolf at
Girton and Newnham colleges, University of Cambridge,
on October 20 and 26 1928.

However, because no copies of the speech were made,
the text used here is taken from Woolf's 1929 essay
A Room of One's Own (Penguin, 1929), which was based on
the talks at Girton and Newnham colleges.

For ease of reading, individual excisions are not marked,
nor is it indicated when the case of a letter changes
due to the deletion of part of a sentence.

Kate Mosse

Kate Mosse is a novelist and co-founder
of the Orange prize for fiction.

Virginia Woolf was a striking woman, the kind of person
you would have noticed. I don't suppose many would have
fixated on the size of her nose as she stood at the front of
the lecture hall (I imagine it packed) – as the media did
when Nicole Kidman dressed down to play her in *The
Hours*.

In October 1928, Woolf gave two talks at the Cambridge
women's colleges of Girton and Newnham under the heading
'Women and Fiction'. Over the following year she reworked
the ideas into a magazine piece and a more substantial
polemic, published as *A Room of One's Own* in October 1929.
As no verbatim record of Woolf's lectures survives, the
speech below is taken from *A Room of One's Own*. It is

unquestionably one of the 20th century's most significant statements on the question of women and writing.

Woolf's central idea, that 'a woman must have money and a room of her own if she is to write fiction', has become a shorthand for the domestic and social obstacles, the pots and pans and poverty, that must be overcome if an artist is to create anything worth the paper it is written on.

So this is not a speech in the same sense that many other pieces in this series are speeches. It is intimate, not public; it is conversational, colloquial, a thinking aloud, rather than a statement designed to be reported by journalists. It is aimed at a literary audience, not the world's media, politicians, watchers. We can't know exactly which of the words included here were first spoken in the lecture halls, but *A Room of One's Own* retains the sense of the spoken word in its brilliant interweaving of personal experience, imaginative musing and political clarity. And it retains the speech-like peroration that was the impassioned call to action for the young women she addressed.

When Woolf gave her Cambridge speeches, feminism seemed becalmed. The breakthrough of women's suffrage and the great cost at which it was achieved had exhausted the movement and given the impression that, perhaps, the job was done. Woolf stood up and asked those uncomfortable questions: why did men drink wine and women water? Why was one sex so prosperous and the other so poor? What effect has poverty on fiction? What are the conditions necessary for the creation of works of art? When every

Elizabethan man seemed 'capable of song or sonnet', how can we explain 'why no woman wrote a word'?

Woolf saw the 'intelligent, eager, poor' undergraduates in front of her as the avengers of Shakespeare's imaginary sister Judith, a bright and ambitious girl who, in her scenario, is driven to commit suicide – as Woolf herself did in 1941 – as a consequence of her desperate attempts to fulfil her creative dreams. Using their own gifts and the liberty given to them, Woolf suggested, the students of 1928 might speak for those to whom that luxury had been denied.

Yet a paradox lies at the heart of the piece. While Woolf exhorts women writers not to allow anger to distort the integrity of their work, the essay itself bristles with anger. Woolf lays bare numerous examples of men's rage against women, their violence, both domestic and literary, their need to ridicule or derogate women's creative achievements in order to bolster their own self-esteem. She contrasts the women who appear in fiction by men with their real-life counterparts, 'locked up, beaten and flung about the room'. Her frustration at being chased from the lawns of an Oxbridge college by a beadle who interrupts her train of thought, at being denied access to the library, at being brought face to face with the misogynist professor in the British Museum, all speak of genuine bitterness at the way women have always been patronised, but also of awareness of the intellectual price paid as a result.

Woolf gives the impression – always, it seems to me – of someone teetering on the brink of revelation. Should she fall, the image will be lost. So she struggles to keep her balance. Her sentences are rangy, with a bouncy emphasis in keeping with their genesis as words intended to be performed. One clause balances another, either side of the fulcrum of a semicolon; not everything needs to be explained, sometimes a juxtaposition is enough. Stepping forward to the podium or to the lectern – I imagine a lectern; there may not have been one – she begins each passage as if resuming a conversation interrupted by having sought shelter from the rain.

Perhaps, today, a lecture of equal importance is taking place at Newnham or Girton. But Virginia Woolf, 1928 . . . How I would love to have been there.

Shakespeare's sister

VIRGINIA WOOLF
October 20 and 26 1928

But, you may say, we asked you to speak about women and fiction – what, has that got to do with a room of one's own? I will try to explain. When you asked me to speak about women and fiction I sat down on the banks of a river and began to wonder what the words meant. They might mean simply a few remarks about Fanny Burney, a few more about Jane Austen, a tribute to the Brontës and a sketch of Haworth Parsonage under snow; some witticisms if possible about Miss Mitford, a respectful allusion to George Eliot; a reference to Mrs Gaskell, and one would have done. But at second sight the words seemed not so simple. The title 'Women and Fiction' might mean, and you may have meant it to mean, women and what they are like, or it might mean women and the fiction that they write, or it might mean women and the fiction that is written about them, or it might mean that somehow all three are inextricably mixed together and you want me to consider them in that light. But when I began to consider the subject in this last way, which seemed the most interesting, I soon saw that it had one fatal drawback: I should never be able to come to a conclusion.

I should never be able to fulfil what is, I understand, the first duty of a lecturer – to hand you, after an hour's discourse, a nugget of pure truth to wrap up between the pages of your notebooks and keep on the mantelpiece for ever. All I could do was to offer you an opinion upon one minor point: a woman must have money and a room of her own if she is to write fiction; and that, as you will see, leaves the great problem of the true nature of woman and the true nature of fiction unsolved. I have shirked the duty of coming to a conclusion upon these two questions; women and fiction remain, so far as I am concerned, unsolved problems.

But in order to make some amends, I am going to do what I can to show you how I arrived at this opinion about the room and the money. I need not say that what I am about to describe has no existence; Oxbridge is an invention; so is Fernham; 'I' is only a convenient term for somebody who has no real being. Lies will flow from my lips, but there may perhaps be some truth mixed up with them; it is for you to seek out this truth and to decide whether any part of it is worth keeping. If not, you will of course throw the whole of it into the wastepaper basket and forget all about it.

Here then was I (call me Mary Beton, Mary Seton, Mary Carmichael or by any name you please – it is not a matter of any importance) sitting on the banks of a river a week or two ago in fine October weather, lost in thought. To the right and left, bushes of some sort, golden and crimson, glowed with the colour – even it seemed burnt with the heat – of fire. On the further bank the willows wept in perpetual lamentation, their hair about their shoulders.

There one might have sat the clock round, lost in thought. Thought – to call it by a prouder name than it deserved – had let its line down into the stream. It swayed, minute after minute, hither and thither among the reflections and the weeds, letting the water lift it and sink it until – you know the little tug – the sudden conglomeration of an idea at the end of one's line: and then the cautious hauling of it in, and the careful laying of it out? Alas, laid on the grass, how small, how insignificant this thought of mine looked; the sort of fish that a good fisherman puts back into the water so that it may grow fatter and be one day worth cooking and eating. I will not trouble you with that thought now, though if you look carefully you may find it for yourselves in the course of what I am going to say.

But however small it was, it had, nevertheless, the mysterious property of its kind – put back into the mind, it became at once very exciting, and important; and as it darted and sank, and flashed hither and thither, set up such a wash and tumult of ideas that it was impossible to sit still. It was thus that I found myself walking with extreme rapidity across a grass plot. Instantly a man's figure rose to intercept me. Nor did I at first understand that the gesticulations of a curious-looking object, in a cutaway coat and evening shirt, were aimed at me. His face expressed horror and indignation. Instinct rather than reason came to my help; he was a beadle, I was a woman. This was the turf; there was the path. Only the fellows and scholars are allowed here; the gravel is the place for me. Such thoughts were the work of a moment. As I regained the path, the arms of the beadle sank, his face assumed its usual repose, and though turf is better walking than gravel, no very great harm was done. The only charge I could bring against the fellows and scholars of whatever the college might happen to be was that, in protection of their turf, which has been rolled for 300 years in succession, they had sent my little fish into hiding.

What idea it had been that had sent me so audaciously trespassing I could not now remember. The spirit of peace descended like a cloud from heaven, for if the spirit of peace dwells anywhere, it is in the courts and quadrangles of Oxbridge on a fine October morning. As chance would have it, some stray memory of some old essay about revisiting Oxbridge in the long vacation brought Charles Lamb to mind – Saint Charles, said Thackeray, putting a letter of Lamb's to his forehead. Indeed, among all the dead (I give you my thoughts as they came to me), Lamb is one of the most congenial; one to whom one would have liked to say, 'Tell me then how you wrote your essays?' For his essays are superior even to Max Beerbohm's, I thought, and started with poetry.

Lamb then came to Oxbridge perhaps 100 years ago.

Certainly he wrote an essay – the name escapes me – about the manuscript of one of Milton's poems which he saw here. It was *Lycidas* perhaps, and Lamb wrote how it shocked him to think it possible that any word in *Lycidas* could have been different from what it is. It then occurred to me that the very manuscript itself which Lamb had looked at was only a few hundred yards away, so that one could follow Lamb's footsteps across the quadrangle to that famous library where the treasure is kept.

But here I was actually at the door which leads into the library itself. I must have opened it, for instantly there issued, like a guardian angel barring the way with a flutter of black gown instead of white wings, a deprecating, silvery, kindly gentleman, who regretted in a low voice as he waved me back that ladies are only admitted to the library if accompanied by a fellow of the college or furnished with a letter of introduction.

The scene, if I may ask you to follow me, was now changed. The leaves were still falling, but in London now, not Oxbridge; and I must ask you to imagine a room, like many thousands, with a window looking across people's hats and vans and motor cars to other windows, and on the table inside the room a blank sheet of paper on which was written in large letters 'WOMEN AND FICTION', but no more. The inevitable sequel to Oxbridge seemed, unfortunately, to be a visit to the British Museum.

Have you any notion of how many books are written about women in the course of one year? Have you any notion how many are written by men? Are you aware that you are, perhaps, the most discussed animal in the universe? Here had I come with a notebook and a pencil proposing to spend a morning reading, supposing that at the end of the morning I should have transferred the truth to my notebook.

But while I pondered, I had unconsciously, in my list-lessness, in my desperation, been drawing a face, a figure. It was the face and the figure of Professor von X engaged in writing his monumental work entitled *The Mental, Moral, and Physical Inferiority of the Female Sex*. He was not in my picture a man attractive to women. He was heavily built; he had a great jowl; to balance that, he had very small eyes; he was very red in the face. His expression suggested that he was labouring under some emotion that made him jab his pen on the paper as if he were killing some noxious insect as he wrote, but even when he had killed it that did not satisfy him; he must go on killing it; and even so, some cause for anger and irritation remained.

Could it be his wife, I asked, looking at my picture? Was she in love with a cavalry officer? Was the cavalry officer slim and elegant and dressed in astrakhan? Had he been laughed at, to adopt the Freudian theory, in his cradle by a pretty girl? For even in his cradle, the professor, I thought, could not have been an attractive child. Whatever the reason, the professor was made to look very angry and very ugly in my sketch, as he wrote his great book upon the mental, moral and physical inferiority of women.

Drawing pictures was an idle way of finishing an

unprofitable morning's work. Yet it is in our idleness, in our dreams, that the submerged truth sometimes comes to the top. A very elementary exercise in psychology showed me, on looking at my notebook, that the sketch of the angry professor had been made in anger. Anger had snatched my pencil while I dreamt. But what was anger doing there? Interest, confusion, amusement, boredom – all these emotions I could trace and name as they succeeded each other throughout the morning. Had anger, the black snake, been lurking among them?

Yes, said the sketch, anger had. It referred me unmistakably to the one book, to the one phrase, which had roused the demon; it was the professor's statement about the mental, moral and physical inferiority of women. My heart had leapt. My cheeks had burnt. I had flushed with anger. There was nothing specially remarkable, however foolish, in that. One does not like to be told that one is naturally the inferior of a little man – I looked at the student next to me – who breathes hard, wears a ready-made tie, and has not shaved this fortnight. One has certain foolish vanities. It is only human nature, I reflected, and began drawing cartwheels and circles over the angry professor's face.

Soon my own anger was explained and done with, but curiosity remained. How explain the anger of the professors? Why were they angry? For when it came to analysing the impression left by these books there was always an element of heat. This heat took many forms; it showed itself in satire, in sentiment, in curiosity, in reprobation. But there was another element which was often present and could not immediately be identified. Anger, I called it.

It was disappointing not to have brought back in the evening some important statement, some authentic fact. Women are poorer than men because . . . this or that. Perhaps now it would be better to give up seeking for the truth, and receiving on one's head an avalanche of opinion hot as lava, discoloured as dishwater. It would be better to draw the curtains; to shut out distractions; to light the lamp; to narrow the enquiry and to ask the historian, who records not opinions but facts, to describe under what conditions women lived, not throughout the ages, but in England, say, in the time of Elizabeth.

For it is a perennial puzzle why no woman wrote a word of that extraordinary literature when every other man, it seemed, was capable of song or sonnet. What were the conditions in which women lived? I asked myself; for fiction, imaginative work that is, is not dropped like a pebble upon the ground, as science may be; fiction is like a spider's web, attached ever so lightly perhaps, but still attached to life at all four corners. Often the attachment is scarcely perceptible; Shakespeare's plays, for instance, seem to hang there complete by themselves. But when the web is pulled askew, hooked up at the edge, torn in the middle, one remembers that these webs are not spun in midair by incorporeal creatures, but are the work of suffering human beings, and are attached to grossly material things, like health and money and the houses we live in.

I went, therefore, to the shelf where the histories stand and took down one of the latest, Professor Trevelyan's *History of England*. Once more I looked up 'Women', found 'position of' and turned to the pages indicated. 'Wife-beating,' I read, 'was a recognised right of man, and was practised without shame by high as well as low ... Similarly,' the historian goes on, 'the daughter who refused to marry the gentleman of her parents' choice was liable to be locked up, beaten and flung about the room, without any shock being inflicted on public opinion.'

I could not help thinking, as I looked at the works of Shakespeare on the shelf, that it would have been impossible, completely and entirely, for any woman to have written the plays of Shakespeare in the age of Shakespeare. Let me imagine, since facts are so hard to come by, what would have happened had Shakespeare had a wonderfully gifted sister, called Judith, let us say. Shakespeare himself went, very probably – his mother was an heiress – to the grammar school, where he may have learnt Latin – Ovid, Virgil and Horace – and the elements of grammar and logic. He was, it is well known, a wild boy who poached rabbits, perhaps shot a deer, and had, rather sooner than he should have done, married a woman in the neighbourhood, who bore him a child rather quicker than was right.

That escapade sent him to seek his fortune in London. He had, it seemed, a taste for the theatre; he began by holding horses at the stage door. Very soon he got work in the theatre, became a successful actor, and lived at the hub of the universe, meeting everybody, knowing everybody, practising his art on the boards, exercising his wits in the streets, and even getting access to the palace of the queen.

Meanwhile, his extraordinarily gifted sister, let us suppose, remained at home. She was as adventurous, as imaginative, as agog to see the world as he was. But she was not sent to school. She had no chance of learning grammar and logic, let alone of reading Horace and Virgil. She picked up a book now and then, one of her brother's perhaps, and read a few pages. But then her parents came in and told her to mend the stockings or mind the stew and not moon about with books and papers. They would have spoken sharply but kindly, for they were substantial people who knew the conditions of life for a woman and loved their daughter – indeed, more likely than not she was the apple of her father's eye.

Perhaps she scribbled some pages up in an apple loft on the sly, but was careful to hide them or set fire to them. Soon, however, before she was out of her teens, she was to be betrothed to the son of a neighbouring woolstapler. She cried out that marriage was hateful to her, and for that she was severely beaten by her father. Then he ceased to scold her. He begged her instead not to hurt him, not to shame him in this matter of her marriage. He would give her a chain of beads or a fine petticoat, he said; and there were tears in his eyes. How could she disobey him? How could she break his heart?

The force of her own gift alone drove her to it. She made

up a small parcel of her belongings, let herself down by a rope one summer's night and took the road to London. She was not 17. The birds that sang in the hedge were not more musical than she was. She had the quickest fancy, a gift like her brother's, for the tune of words. Like him, she had a taste for the theatre. She stood at the stage door; she wanted to act, she said. Men laughed in her face. The manager – a fat, looselipped man – guffawed. He bellowed something about poodles dancing and women acting – no woman, he said, could possibly be an actress. He hinted – you can imagine what. She could get no training in her craft. Could she even seek her dinner in a tavern or roam the streets at midnight?

Yet her genius was for fiction and lusted to feed abundantly upon the lives of men and women and the study of their ways. At last – for she was very young, oddly like Shakespeare the poet in her face, with the same grey eyes – at last the actor-manager took pity on her; she found herself with child by that gentleman and so – who shall measure the heat and violence of the poet's heart when caught and tangled in a woman's body? – killed herself one winter's night and lies buried at some crossroads where the omnibuses now stop outside the Elephant and Castle.

Here, then, Mary Beton ceases to speak. She has asked you to follow her flying into the arms of a beadle, drawing pictures in the British Museum, taking books from the shelf, looking out of the window. While she has been doing all these things, you no doubt have been observing her failings and foibles and deciding what effect they have had on her opinions. You have been contradicting her and making whatever additions and deductions seem good to you. That is all as it should be, for in a question like this truth, is only to be had by laying together many varieties of error.

Here I would stop, but the pressure of convention decrees that every speech must end with a peroration. And a peroration addressed to women should have something, you will agree, particularly exalting and ennobling about it. I should implore you to remember your responsibilities, to be higher, more spiritual; I should remind you how much depends upon you, and what an influence you can exert upon the future. But those exhortations can safely, I think, be left to the other sex, who will put them, and indeed have put them, with far greater eloquence than I can compass. When I rummage in my own mind I find no noble sentiments about being companions and equals and influencing the world to higher ends. I find myself saying briefly and prosaically that it is much more important to be oneself than anything else. Do not dream of influencing other people, I would say, if I knew how to make it sound exalted. Think of things in themselves.

How can I further encourage you to go about the business of life? Young women, I would say – and please attend, for the peroration is beginning – you are, in my opinion, disgracefully ignorant. You have never made a discovery of any sort of importance. You have never shaken an empire or led an army into battle. The plays of Shakespeare are not by you, and you have never introduced a barbarous race to the blessings of civilisation. What is your excuse?

It is all very well for you to say, pointing to the streets and squares and forests of the globe swarming with black and white and coffee-coloured inhabitants, all busily engaged in traffic and enterprise and love-making, we have had other work on our hands. Without our doing, those seas would be unsailed and those fertile lands a desert. We have borne and bred and washed and taught, perhaps to the age of six or seven years, the 1,623,000,000 human beings who are, according to statistics, at present in existence, and that, allowing that some had help, takes time.

There is truth in what you say – I will not deny it. But at the same time may I remind you that there have been at least two colleges for women in existence in England since the year 1866; that after the year 1880 a married woman was allowed by law to possess her own property; and that in 1919 – which is a whole nine years ago – she was given a vote? May I also remind you that most of the professions have been open to you for close on 10 years now? When you reflect upon these immense privileges and the length of time during which they have been enjoyed, and the fact that there must be at this moment some 2,000 women capable of earning over £500 a year in one way or another, you will agree that the excuse of lack of opportunity, training, encouragement, leisure and money no longer holds good.

A thousand pens are ready to suggest what you should do and what effect you will have. My own suggestion is a little fantastic, I admit; I prefer, therefore, to put it in the form of fiction. I told you in the course of this paper that Shakespeare had a sister; but do not look for her in Sir Sidney Lee's life of the poet. She died young – alas, she never wrote a word. She lies buried where the omnibuses now stop, opposite the Elephant and Castle. Now my belief is that this poet who never wrote a word and was buried at the crossroads still lives. She lives in you and in me, and in many other women who are not here tonight, for they are washing up the dishes and putting the children to bed. But she lives, for great poets do not die; they are continuing presences; they need only the opportunity to walk among us in the flesh.

This opportunity, as I think, it is now coming within your power to give her. For my belief is that if we live another century or so – I am talking of the common life which is the real life and not of the little separate lives which we live as individuals – and have £500 a year each of us and rooms of our own; if we have the habit of freedom and the courage to write exactly what we think; if we escape a little from the common sitting-room and see human beings not always in their relation to each other but in relation to reality; and the sky too, and the trees or whatever it may be in themselves; if we face the fact, for it is a fact, that there is no arm to cling to, but that we go alone and that our relation is to the world of reality and not only to the world of men and women, then the opportunity will come and the dead poet who was Shakespeare's sister will put on the body which she has so often laid down. Drawing her life from the lives of the unknown who were her forerunners, as her brother did before her, she will be born.

As for her coming without that preparation, without that effort on our part, without that determination that when she is born again she shall find it possible to live and write her poetry, that we cannot expect, for that would he impossible. But I maintain that she would come if we worked for her, and that so to work, even in poverty and obscurity, is worthwhile.

Speech copyright © The Society of Authors, as the literary representative of the estate of Virginia Woolf.

The *Manchester Guardian* did not report Virginia
Woolf's talks at Cambridge. This piece, from *The New
York Times* on November 10 1929, is a review of
Woolf's essay, based on the talks.

VIRGINIA WOOLF DISCUSSES
WOMEN AND FICTION
A room of one's own

By Louis Kronenberger

Asked to speak at Cambridge on the subject 'Women and Fiction'
– for this was a lecture before it was an essay – Mrs Woolf
confessed that the subject could encompass a great deal. But
on reflection she saw that all she could do was to offer you
an opinion upon one minor point – a woman must have money
and a room of her own if she is to write fiction.

Having so clearly indicated her argument, Mrs Woolf
even more clearly proceeds to maintain and illuminate it.
She says little that has not been said before; but seldom has
the point been driven home more cogently or embellished
with wittier comment.

With the inherent taste of a novelist, Mrs Woolf chooses
to speak through an 'I' who is and yet is not herself, and to
enforce her argument through incident. This slightly fictional
setting tends to impersonalize Mrs Woolf's attitude at the

same time that it gives artificial personality to her remarks and breaks up a purely historical analysis with running comment – and with, it must be admitted, some highly irrelevant passages of description.

Achievements

What Mrs Woolf has traced, of course, are the reasons for the very limited achievements among women novelists through the centuries. Why did they fail? They failed because they were not financially independent; they failed because they were not intellectually free; they failed because they were denied the fullest worldly experience.

Mrs Woolf imagines what would have happened to a hypothetical sister of Shakespeare (who possessed all his genius); she insists that, whatever her gifts, no woman in that age of wife-beating could have written the plays. But even within the limits of their own possibilities in past times, Mrs Woolf continues, women did not find themselves because they wrote in deference to masculine standards or in angry defiance of them.

Thus Mrs Woolf has traced the position of the woman writer through the centuries, wittily finishing it off with contrasting pictures of men's lives and women's lives even today. We have summarized baldly, whereas Mrs Woolf speaks for her sex with as much fancy as logic, as much wit as knowledge, and with the imagination of a true novelist. And she speaks for it well.

Special plea

Moreover, she escapes from an attitude of conventional feminism by really arguing in this book not for women but for artists. For all artists, whatever their sex, need 500 pounds a year and a room of their own. It is only because women have had them so much less frequently than men that a special plea for them has a special force.

In making that plea Mrs Woolf sometimes partly evades an issue. We cannot tell how much better Dickens would have written had he not struggled, or Meredith had he not wearily read manuscripts for Chapman & Hall, or Balzac had he not sought feverishly to discharge heavy debts; but we do know that lacking means and intellectual freedom, these men succeeded where women failed. We cannot tell how much better Hawthorne would have written, or Flaubert, or Hardy, had their experiences been more cosmopolitan; but we do know that great knowledge of the world is not necessary for great art. Jane Austen knew nobody and George Sand knew everybody, and Jane Austen was by far the greater.

But in spite of a theme that is pretty self-evident and conclusions that are not always definitive, this book, the distillation of the crystalline mind, so gaily and freshly and yet forcefully written, says something. Many of the best things are said in passing – flashes of insight, succinct bits of criticism, the significant touches which always mark the writer who knows a great deal more than the one thing he is commissioned to discuss.

Occasionally Mrs Woolf is not above sacrificing the truth to wit, or impartial judgment to a tempting thrust. But nearly always, even at her most informal, she maintains an unfaltering poise.

The only thing we have to fear is fear itself

Franklin D Roosevelt
March 4 1933

This speech was delivered by Franklin D Roosevelt
at his inauguration in Washington on March 4 1933.

Gordon Brown

Gordon Brown is the Prime Minister.

Do words have power? It was, as Franklin D Roosevelt said, 'a stricken nation' that he was addressing for the first time as president – a nation of closed banks, shut down factories, shattered confidence and millions without work or hope. He left his wheelchair, in which he was seldom if ever seen in public, inside the Capitol building and descended the steps outside to the inaugural platform, supported by steel braces and the steadying arm of one of his sons. It was a chill, overcast March day. But as his powerful cadences reverberated across the vast throng and on radio across a vast continental expanse, this man who could not walk unaided lifted a great and prostrate nation to its feet.

Before the 1932 election the legendary columnist Walter

Lippmann described FDR as: 'an amiable man . . . without very strong convictions'. 'He is no tribune of the people; he is no enemy of entrenched privilege. He is a pleasant man who, without any important qualifications for the office, would very much like to be president.' Sometimes even the best of the press gets it utterly wrong. From the first lines of this speech, lifted to the heights by Roosevelt's famous cry – 'The only thing we have to fear is fear itself' – America knew that here was a lion of a leader, an aristocrat who would fight for 'the forgotten man'. As he spoke of 'action and action now', the dark clouds began to lift – literally from the skies of Washington, and in the hearts of Americans.

Roosevelt did not offer a detailed programme. The old order had collapsed; the old certitudes were as bankrupt as the countless companies that had gone under. Roosevelt did not know exactly what to do. He would try a policy and, if it failed, try again until he found something that worked. He would discard one of the clearest pledges of this inaugural speech – that the cost of government would be 'drastically reduced' – when he saw that the only way forward was for government to stimulate the economy, invest in great public works, feed the hungry and for a time employ millions who had nowhere else to turn. This was denounced as 'make work', but to Roosevelt, it was better than no work. His trusted adviser Harry Hopkins explained that people don't eat in the long run; they eat every day – or starve in the long run. So Roosevelt was a pragmatist: yet he was guided by an idealism that reflected his instinctive sense of the common good and the fair society. Along with the gleaming phrases and the optimism that this speech radiated, it also expressed timeless ideals: 'social values more noble than mere monetary profit', honour in place of 'callous and selfish wrongdoing', a trust in 'the future of essential democracy'.

So on March 4 1933, Americans saw and heard for the first time in their new president what he pledged that day and what others across the globe would come to know in the dark days of the second world war – 'courage and the devotion that befit the time'.

Abraham Lincoln was great because he saved America's union during a civil war. Roosevelt, the happy warrior of the political battlefield, ranks in American history just behind him; he saved the economic system and perhaps even the democratic institutions of the US. Then, for his country and the world, he played an indispensable part, side by side with his friend and fellow giant Winston Churchill, in saving freedom from the nightmare of fascism.

On March 4 1933, he was a prophet of the American dream who summoned his fellow citizens to confront the 'nameless, unreasoning, unjustified terror which paralyses needed efforts to convert retreat into advance'. He 'boldly' asserted that 'this great nation will endure, as it has endured, will revive and will prosper.'

And there was no time to wait. FDR's inaugural address signalled the start of an onrushing period, a sweep of legislation that transformed America; then and in the years that followed, he reformed the free market and rebalanced it with the welfare state.

It was one of those rare speeches that in themselves change the course of events. These great words were great works that altered the consciousness of a nation. President Roosevelt would grapple with depression in the economy as the recovery he brought yielded again in 1937 to a recession that did not finally end until the outbreak of war. But in his first half hour, on that inaugural platform, his eloquence ended once and for all the more profound depression of national spirit that had afflicted and paralysed America. These words had the power to move America. And they have an imperishable power to move us all.

The only thing we have to fear is fear itself

Franklin D Roosevelt
March 4 1933

President Hoover, Mr Chief Justice, my friends: This is a day of national consecration. And I am certain that on this day my fellow Americans expect that on my induction into the presidency, I will address them with a candour and a decision which the present situation of our people impels.

This is preeminently the time to speak the truth, the whole truth, frankly and boldly. Nor need we shrink from honestly facing conditions in our country today. This great nation will endure, as it has endured, will revive and will prosper. So, first of all, let me assert my firm belief that the only thing we have to fear is fear itself – nameless, unreasoning, unjustified terror which paralyses needed efforts to convert retreat into advance. In every dark hour of our national life, a leadership of frankness and of vigour has met with that understanding and support of the people themselves which is essential to victory. And I am convinced that you will again give that support to leadership in these critical days.

In such a spirit on my part and on yours we face our common difficulties. They concern, thank God, only material things. Values have shrunk to fantastic levels; taxes have risen; our ability to pay has fallen; government of all kinds is faced by serious curtailment of income; the means of exchange are frozen in the currents of trade; the withered leaves of industrial enterprise lie on every side; farmers find no markets for their produce; and the savings of many years in thousands of families are gone. More important, a host of unemployed citizens face the grim problem of existence, and an equally great number toil with little return. Only a foolish optimist can deny the dark realities of the moment.

And yet our distress comes from no failure of substance. We are stricken by no plague of locusts. Compared with the perils which our forefathers conquered, because they believed and were not afraid, we have still much to be thankful for. Nature still offers her bounty and human efforts have multiplied it. Plenty is at our doorstep, but a generous use of it languishes in the very sight of the supply.

Primarily, this is because the rulers of the exchange of mankind's goods have failed, through their own stubbornness and their own incompetence, have admitted their failure, and have abdicated. Practices of the unscrupulous money changers stand indicted in the court of public opinion, rejected by the hearts and minds of men.

True, they have tried. But their efforts have been cast in the pattern of an outworn tradition. Faced by failure of credit, they have proposed only the lending of more money.

Stripped of the lure of profit by which to induce our people to follow their false leadership, they have resorted to exhortations, pleading tearfully for restored confidence. They only know the rules of a generation of self-seekers. They have no vision, and when there is no vision the people perish.

Yes, the money changers have fled from their high seats in the temple of our civilisation. We may now restore that temple to the ancient truths. The measure of that restoration lies in the extent to which we apply social values more noble than mere monetary profit.

Happiness lies not in the mere possession of money; it lies in the joy of achievement, in the thrill of creative effort. The joy, the moral stimulation of work no longer must be forgotten in the mad chase of evanescent profits. These dark days, my friends, will be worth all they cost us if they teach us that our true destiny is not to be ministered unto but to minister to ourselves, to our fellow men.

Recognition of that falsity of material wealth as the standard of success goes hand in hand with the abandonment of the false belief that public office and high political position are to be valued only by the standards of pride of place and personal profit; and there must be an end to a conduct in banking and in business which too often has given to a sacred trust the likeness of callous and selfish wrongdoing. Small wonder that confidence languishes, for it thrives only on honesty, on honour, on the sacredness of obligations, on faithful protection, and on unselfish performance; without them it cannot live.

Restoration calls, however, not for changes in ethics alone. This nation is asking for action, and action now.

Our greatest primary task is to put people to work. This is no unsolvable problem if we face it wisely and courageously. It can be accomplished in part by direct recruiting by the government itself, treating the task as we would treat the emergency of a war, but at the same time, through this employment, accomplishing greatly needed projects to stimulate and reorganise the use of our great natural resources.

Hand in hand with that we must frankly recognise the overbalance of population in our industrial centres and, by engaging on a national scale in a redistribution, endeavour to provide a better use of the land for those best fitted for the land.

Yes, the task can be helped by definite efforts to raise the values of agricultural products, and with this the power to purchase the output of our cities. It can be helped by preventing realistically the tragedy of the growing loss through foreclosure of our small homes and our farms. It can be helped by insistence that the federal, the state, and the local governments act forthwith on the demand that their cost be drastically reduced. It can be helped by the unifying of relief activities which today are often scattered, uneconomical, unequal. It can be helped by national planning for and supervision of all forms of transportation and of communications and other utilities that have a definitely public character.

There are many ways in which it can be helped, but it can never be helped by merely talking about it.

We must act. We must act quickly. And finally, in our progress towards a resumption of work, we require two safeguards against a return of the evils of the old order. There must be a strict supervision of all banking and credits and investments. There must be an end to speculation with other people's money. And there must be provision for an adequate but sound currency.

These, my friends, are the lines of attack. I shall presently urge upon a new Congress in special session detailed measures for their fulfillment, and I shall seek the immediate assistance of the 48 states.

Through this programme of action we address ourselves to putting our own national house in order and making income balance outgo. Our international trade relations, though vastly important, are in point of time, and necessity, secondary to the establishment of a sound national economy. I favour, as a practical policy, the putting of first things first. I shall spare no effort to restore world trade by international economic readjustment; but the emergency at home cannot wait on that accomplishment.

The basic thought that guides these specific means of national recovery is not narrowly nationalistic. It is the insistence, as a first consideration, upon the interdependence of the various elements in and parts of the United States of America – a recognition of the old and permanently important manifestation of the American spirit of the pioneer. It is the way to recovery. It is the immediate way. It is the strongest assurance that recovery will endure.

In the field of world policy, I would dedicate this nation to the policy of the good neighbour: the neighbour who resolutely respects himself and, because he does so, respects the rights of others; the neighbour who respects his obligations and respects the sanctity of his agreements in and with a world of neighbours.

If I read the temper of our people correctly, we now realise, as we have never realised before, our interdependence on each other; that we can not merely take, but we must give as well; that if we are to go forward, we must move as a trained and loyal army willing to sacrifice for the good of a common discipline, because without such discipline no progress can be made, no leadership becomes effective.

We are, I know, ready and willing to submit our lives and our property to such discipline, because it makes possible a leadership which aims at the larger good. This, I propose to offer, pledging that the larger purposes will bind upon us, bind upon us all as a sacred obligation with a unity of duty hitherto evoked only in times of armed strife. With this pledge taken, I assume unhesitatingly the leadership of this great army of our people dedicated to a disciplined attack upon our common problems.

Action in this image, action to this end is feasible under the form of government which we have inherited from our ancestors. Our constitution is so simple, so practical that it is possible always to meet extraordinary needs by changes in emphasis and arrangement without loss of essential form.

That is why our constitutional system has proved itself the most superbly enduring political mechanism the modern world has ever seen.

It has met every stress of vast expansion of territory, of foreign wars, of bitter internal strife, of world relations. And it is to be hoped that the normal balance of executive and legislative authority may be wholly equal, wholly adequate to meet the unprecedented task before us. But it may be that an unprecedented demand and need for undelayed action may call for temporary departure from that normal balance of public procedure.

I am prepared under my constitutional duty to recommend the measures that a stricken nation in the midst of a stricken world may require. These measures, or such other measures as the Congress may build out of its experience and wisdom, I shall seek, within my constitutional authority, to bring to speedy adoption.

But, in the event that the Congress shall fail to take one of these two courses, in the event that the national emergency is still critical, I shall not evade the clear course of duty that will then confront me. I shall ask the Congress for the one remaining instrument to meet the crisis – broad executive power to wage a war against the emergency, as great as the power that would be given to me if we were in fact invaded by a foreign foe.

For the trust reposed in me, I will return the courage and the devotion that befit the time. I can do no less.

We face the arduous days that lie before us in the warm

courage of national unity; with the clear consciousness of seeking old and precious moral values; with the clean satisfaction that comes from the stern performance of duty by old and young alike. We aim at the assurance of a rounded and permanent national life.

We do not distrust the future of essential democracy. The people of the United States have not failed. In their need they have registered a mandate that they want direct, vigorous action. They have asked for discipline and direction under leadership. They have made me the present instrument of their wishes. In the spirit of the gift I take it.

In this dedication of a nation, we humbly ask the blessing of God.

May He protect each and every one of us.

May He guide me in the days to come.

Following the Saturday inauguration, this report ran in the *Manchester Guardian* on Monday March 6 1933.

MR ROOSEVELT TAKES OFFICE
Outlines of the 'new deal': his views on currencies

From our own correspondent, New York

President Franklin D Roosevelt threw down the gauntlet to depression in the inaugural address he delivered immediately after he took the oath of office at the Capitol yesterday. Declaring that the 'only thing we have to fear is fear itself', he promised an unflagging struggle against the difficulties in which the United States finds itself.

With almost every bank in the country closed, he warned the nation and Congress that he would ask for wartime dictatorial powers if necessary 'as great as the power that would be given me if we were in fact invaded by a foreign foe.' He denounced in vigorous terms the past policies of some American bankers for 'stubbornness and incompetence' saying:

'The money-changers have fled from their high seats in the temple of our civilisation. We may now restore that temple to the ancient truths.'

The new President declared for 'adequate but sound' currency, a phrase which was interpreted by both the advocates of limited inflation and the deflationists as supporting their views.

The 'new deal'

He gave a brief outline of some aspects of his famous 'new deal' along the lines foreshadowed by his campaign addresses. He strongly hinted at a huge public works programme by the Federal Government to relieve depression and give employment. He advocated a redistribution of the population, with greater emphasis on agriculture and raising the prices of farm products. He pledged himself to reduce the cost of government, to a strict supervision of banking, and endeavours to assist world trade by economic adjustments. He deliberately minimised foreign affairs on the ground that the domestic crisis comes first.

The inauguration ceremonies, which are usually the country's most colourful public spectacle, were somewhat dampened by the knowledge of the crisis through which the country is passing, but they were attended by enormous and enthusiastic crowds.

Mr Roosevelt, who was staying at a Washington hotel, drove to the White House with his wife about eleven o'clock, and joined President and Mrs Hoover for the ride to the Capitol. Here Mr Hoover signed some last minute bills and both men attended the swearing-in of the new senators and the new Vice President, Mr John Garner.

About one o'clock Mr Hoover and Mr Roosevelt, accompanied by their aides, left the Capitol and appeared on the steps of the east portico, where a crowd of perhaps 150,000 persons awaited them. The oath of office was administered by the Chief Justice, Mr Hughes, of the United States Supreme Court, and Mr Roosevelt then delivered his address. He left immediately afterwards for the White House, where he attended the swearing-in of his Cabinet and plunged at once into the consideration of the banking crisis.

Mr Hoover's departure

Mr and Mrs Hoover and their family left immediately by the New York train. Mrs Hoover changed trains at Philadelphia en route for Palo Alto, California, her home. Mr Hoover came to New York, where he will remain for a few days attending to private business and if necessary lending aid in the banking emergency.

The universal comment was that while Mr Roosevelt was ebulliently happy Mr Hoover was tremendously downcast. Tears stood in his eyes as he waved a farewell to the throng at the Washington Railway Station.

We shall fight
on the beaches

WINSTON CHURCHILL
June 4 1940

This speech was delivered to the
House of Commons on June 4 1940.

Simon Schama

Simon Schama is a historian and
contributor to the *Guardian*.

For most of his career, Churchill's grandiloquence was thought
a symptom of his showy shallowness, his inconstancy, his
addiction to hyperbole. But in the catastrophic late spring
of 1940, a lifetime of rhetorical education and mercurial
performance finally paid off. Churchill's words went to war
when Britain's armed forces seemed to be going under.

Though he felt 'physically sick' at the cabinet meeting of
May 26 when the horrifying magnitude of the German sweep
to the Channel was sinking in, Churchill was adamant there
would be no compromise. When Kenneth Clark proposed
taking the cream of the National Gallery's collection to
Canada, Churchill shot back, 'No. Bury them in caves and
cellars. None must go. We are going to beat them.'

The rehearsal for his great performance at Westminster on June 4 was to the full cabinet in which Churchill, passionately declaimed, 'We shall go on and we shall fight it out, here or elsewhere, and if at the last the long story is to end, it were better it should end, not through surrender but only when we are rolling senseless on the ground.' Ministers thumped fists on the table; some rose and patted him on the back. Defeatism – for the moment – had been held at bay. The speech to the House of Commons a week later was meant to pre-empt any further thought of compromise with the 'Nahzies' (a calculatedly dismissive pronunciation) and to turn the mood of the country from despair to resolution. Josiah Wedgwood thought it was worth 'a thousand guns and the speeches of a thousand years' and he was right. It embodied both ethos (noble candour) and pathos (vehement passion) in equal degree and its inspirational persuasion depended fundamentally on one rhetorical tactic: honesty.

Unusually, Churchill dispensed with an introduction and went straight to his narrative of the German blitzkrieg, as if he were writing one of his military histories. No one minded the mixed metaphor 'the German eruption swept like a sharp scythe'. Interspersed in the lengthy story telling was heroic relief, albeit in tragic mood: the futile four days of resistance in Calais (ordered by him). Then followed, in Churchill's archaic manner, 'hard and heavy tidings' of the encirclement. He trowelled on the despair: 'The whole root and core and brain of the British army . . . seemed about to

66

perish upon the field.' But then came the 'miracle of deliverance' account of Dunkirk for which Churchill switched tenses, emulating the chorus from Henry V. 'Suddenly the scene has cleared, the crash and thunder has for the moment . . . died away.' 'Wars are not won by evacuations,' he cautions but then follows another of his romances of the 'island home'; the valiant RAF.

Each time Churchill appeared to be describing calamity, he made sure to punctuate it with gestures of improbable defiance. He could not guarantee there would be no invasion, but he summoned up Clio again to remind the House that Napoleon too had been a victim of that delusion. Even that might have gone differently had the winds in the Channel veered differently. As the great speech moved to its unforgettable peroration, Churchill was giving all who heard it and beyond the sense of historical vocation, a calling against tyranny.

To hear the recording of the speech is to be amazed all over again at the fine tuning of the performance: Churchill deliberately lowers his pitch for much of the 'we shall fight' repetitions, in softly heroic lament, a reproach, perhaps, to the unhinged vocal histrionics of his arch-enemy. Only with 'we shall never surrender' did the voice suddenly produce a mighty Churchillian roar; the full-throated resonance of the roused beast. It's still easy to conjure him up: the glasses down the nose; bottom lip protruding, shoulders stooped, his very un-Ciceronian body language of patting both hands, all five fingers extended, against his chest, then, as Harold Nicolson reported, down his stomach all the way to his groin.

Standing like that, Nicolson wrote he looked like 'a stolid, obstinate ploughman' as if the earth of Britain itself defied the worst that Hitler could throw at it. Nicolson's wife, Vita Sackville-West, wrote to him that even when recited by a news announcer the speech sent 'shivers down my spine'. One of the reason, she wrote, 'why one is stirred by [his] Elizabethan phrases is that one feels the whole massive backing of power and resolve behind them, like a fortress: they are never words for words' sake'. She was right. They were words for everyone's sake. They were the lifeboat and the blood transfusion. They turned the tide.

We shall fight
on the beaches

WINSTON CHURCHILL
June 4 1940

From the moment that the French defences at Sedan and
on the Meuse were broken at the end of the second week
of May, only a rapid retreat to Amiens and the south could
have saved the British and French armies who had entered
Belgium at the appeal of the Belgian king; but this strategic
fact was not immediately realised. The French high command
hoped they would be able to close the gap, and the armies
of the north were under their orders. Moreover, a retirement of this kind would have involved almost certainly the
destruction of the fine Belgian army of over 20 divisions
and the abandonment of the whole of Belgium. Therefore,
when the force and scope of the German penetration were
realised and when a new French generalissimo, General
Weygand, assumed command in place of General Gamelin,
an effort was made by the French and British armies in
Belgium to keep on holding the right hand of the Belgians
and to give their own right hand to a newly created French

army, which was to have advanced across the Somme in great strength to grasp it.

However, the German eruption swept like a sharp scythe around the right and rear of the armies of the north. Eight or nine armoured divisions, each of about 400 armoured vehicles of different kinds, but carefully assorted to be complementary and divisible into small self-contained units, cut off all communications between us and the main French armies. It severed our own communications for food and ammunition, which ran first to Amiens and afterwards through Abbeville, and it shore its way up the coast to Boulogne and Calais, and almost to Dunkirk. Behind this armoured and mechanised onslaught came a number of German divisions in lorries, and behind them again there plodded comparatively slowly the dull brute mass of the ordinary German army and German people, always so ready to be led to the trampling down in other lands of liberties and comforts which they have never known in their own.

I have said this armoured scythe-stroke almost reached Dunkirk – almost but not quite. Boulogne and Calais were the scenes of desperate fighting. The Guards defended Boulogne for a while and were then withdrawn by orders from this country. The Rifle Brigade, the 60th Rifles, and the Queen Victoria's Rifles, with a battalion of British tanks and 1,000 Frenchmen, in all about 4,000 strong, defended Calais to the last. The British brigadier was given an hour to surrender. He spurned the offer, and four days of intense street fighting passed before silence reigned over Calais, which marked the end of a memorable resistance. Only 30 unwounded survivors were brought off by the navy, and we do not know the fate of their comrades. Their sacrifice, however, was not in vain. At least two armoured divisions, which otherwise would have been turned against the British Expeditionary Force, had to be sent to overcome them. They have added another page to the glories of the light divisions, and the time gained enabled the Graveline water lines to be flooded and to be held by the French troops.

Thus it was that the port of Dunkirk was kept open. When it was found impossible for the armies of the north to reopen their communications to Amiens with the main French armies, only one choice remained. It seemed, indeed, forlorn. The Belgian, British and French armies were almost surrounded. Their sole line of retreat was to a single port and to its neighbouring beaches. They were pressed on every side by heavy attacks and far outnumbered in the air.

When, a week ago today, I asked the House to fix this afternoon as the occasion for a statement, I feared it would be my hard lot to announce the greatest military disaster in our long history. I thought – and some good judges agreed with me – that perhaps 20,000 or 30,000 men might be re-embarked. But it certainly seemed that the whole of the French first army and the whole of the British Expeditionary Force north of the Amiens-Abbeville gap would be broken up in the open field or else would have to capitulate for lack of food and ammunition. These were the hard and heavy tidings for which I called upon the

House and the nation to prepare themselves a week ago.
The whole root and core and brain of the British army, on
which and around which we were to build, and are to build,
the great British armies in the later years of the war, seemed
about to perish upon the field or to be led into an igno-
minious and starving captivity.

That was the prospect a week ago. But another blow,
which might well have proved final, was yet to fall upon us.
The king of the Belgians had called upon us to come to his
aid. Had not this ruler and his government severed themselves from the allies, who rescued their country from
extinction in the late war, and had they not sought refuge
in what was proved to be a fatal neutrality, the French and
British armies might well at the outset have saved not only
Belgium but perhaps even Poland. Yet at the last moment,
when Belgium was already invaded, King Leopold called
upon us to come to his aid, and even at the last moment
we came. He and his brave, efficient army, nearly half a
million strong, guarded our left flank and thus kept open
our only line of retreat to the sea. Suddenly, without prior
consultation, with the least possible notice, without the advice
of his ministers and upon his own personal act, he sent a
plenipotentiary to the German command, surrendered his
army, and exposed our whole flank and means of retreat.

I asked the House a week ago to suspend its judgment
because the facts were not clear, but I do not feel that any
reason now exists why we should not form our own opinions upon this pitiful episode. The surrender of the Belgian

army compelled the British at the shortest notice to cover a flank to the sea more than 30 miles in length. Otherwise all would have been cut off, and all would have shared the fate to which King Leopold had condemned the finest army his country had ever formed. So in doing this and in exposing this flank, as anyone who followed the operations on the map will see, contact was lost between the British and two out of the three corps forming the first French army, who were still farther from the coast than we were, and it seemed impossible that any large number of allied troops could reach the coast.

The enemy attacked on all sides with great strength and fierceness, and their main power, the power of their far more numerous air force, was thrown into the battle or else concentrated upon Dunkirk and the beaches. Pressing in upon the narrow exit, both from the east and from the west, the enemy began to fire with cannon upon the beaches by which alone the shipping could approach or depart. They sowed magnetic mines in the channels and seas; they sent repeated waves of hostile aircraft, sometimes more than 100 strong in one formation, to cast their bombs upon the single pier that remained, and upon the sand dunes upon which the troops had their eyes for shelter. Their U-boats, one of which was sunk, and their motor launches took their toll of the vast traffic which now began. For four or five days an intense struggle reigned. All their armoured divisions – or what was left of them – together with great masses of infantry and artillery, hurled themselves in vain upon the ever-narrowing, ever-contracting appendix within which the British and French armies fought.

Meanwhile, the Royal Navy, with the willing help of countless merchant seamen, strained every nerve to embark the British and allied troops; 220 light warships and 650 other vessels were engaged. They had to operate upon the difficult coast, often in adverse weather, under an almost ceaseless hail of bombs and an increasing concentration of artillery fire. Nor were the seas, as I have said, themselves free from mines and torpedoes. It was in conditions such as these that our men carried on, with little or no rest, for days and nights on end, making trip after trip across the dangerous waters, bringing with them always men whom they had rescued. The numbers they have brought back are the measure of their devotion and their courage. The hospital ships, which brought off many thousands of British and French wounded, being so plainly marked were a special target for Nazi bombs; but the men and women on board them never faltered in their duty.

Meanwhile, the Royal Air Force, which had already been intervening in the battle, so far as its range would allow, from home bases, now used part of its main metropolitan fighter strength, and struck at the German bombers and at the fighters which in large numbers protected them. This struggle was protracted and fierce. Suddenly the scene has cleared, the crash and thunder has for the moment – but only for the moment – died away. A miracle of deliverance, achieved by valour, by perseverance, by perfect discipline, by faultless service, by resource, by skill, by unconquerable fidelity, is manifest to us all. The enemy was hurled back by the retreating British and French troops. He was so roughly handled that he did not hurry their departure seriously. The Royal Air Force engaged the main strength of the German air force, and inflicted upon them losses of at least four to one; and the navy, using nearly 1,000 ships of all kinds, carried over 335,000 men, French and British, out of the jaws of death and shame, to their native land and to the tasks which lie immediately ahead. We must be very careful not to assign to this deliverance the attributes of a victory. Wars are not won by evacuations. But there was a victory inside this deliverance, which should be noted. It was gained by the air force. Many of our soldiers coming back have not seen the air force at work; they saw only the bombers which escaped its protective attack. They underrate its achievements. I have heard much talk of this; that is why I go out of my way to say this. I will tell you about it.

This was a great trial of strength between the British and German air forces. Can you conceive a greater objective for the Germans in the air than to make evacuation from these beaches impossible, and to sink all these ships which were displayed, almost to the extent of thousands? Could there have been an objective of greater military importance and significance for the whole purpose of the war than this? They tried hard, and they were beaten back; they were frustrated in their task. We got the army away; and they have paid fourfold for any losses which they have inflicted. Very large formations of German aeroplanes – and we know that they are a very brave race – have turned on several occasions from the attack of one-quarter of their number of the Royal Air Force, and have dispersed in different directions. Twelve aeroplanes have been hunted by two. One aeroplane was driven into the water and cast away by the mere charge of a British aeroplane, which had no more ammunition. All of our types – the Hurricane, the Spitfire and the new Defiant – and all our pilots have been vindicated as superior to what they have at present to face.

When we consider how much greater would be our advantage in defending the air above this island against an overseas attack, I must say that I find in these facts a sure basis upon which practical and reassuring thoughts may rest. I will pay my tribute to these young airmen. The great French army was very largely, for the time being, cast back and disturbed by the onrush of a few thousands of armoured vehicles. May it not also be that the cause of civilisation itself will be defended by the skill and devotion of a few thousand airmen? There never has been, I suppose, in all the world, in all the history of war, such an opportunity for youth. The Knights of the Round Table, the Crusaders, all fall back into the past – not only distant but prosaic; these young men, going forth every morn to guard their native land and all that we stand for, holding in their hands these instruments of colossal and shattering power, of whom it may be said that:

Every morn brought forth a noble chance,
And every chance brought forth a noble knight,

deserve our gratitude, as do all the brave men who, in so many ways and on so many occasions, are ready, and continue ready to give life and all for their native land.

I return to the army. In the long series of very fierce battles, now on this front, now on that, fighting on three fronts at once, battles fought by two or three divisions against an equal or somewhat larger number of the enemy, and fought fiercely on some of the old grounds that so many of us knew so well − in these battles our losses in men have exceeded 30,000 killed, wounded and missing. I take occasion to express the sympathy of the House to all who have suffered bereavement or who are still anxious. The president of the Board of Trade [Sir Andrew Duncan] is not here today. His son has been killed, and many in the House have felt the pangs of affliction in the sharpest form. But I will say this about the missing: We have had a large number of wounded come home safely to this country, but I would say about the missing that there may be very many reported missing who will come back home, some day, in one way or another. In the confusion of this fight it is inevitable that many have been left in positions where honour required no further resistance from them.

Against this loss of over 30,000 men, we can set a far heavier loss certainly inflicted upon the enemy. But our losses in material are enormous. We have perhaps lost one-third of the men we lost in the opening days of the battle of March 21 1918, but we have lost nearly as many guns – nearly 1,000 – and all our transport, all the armoured vehicles that were with the army in the north. This loss will impose a further delay on the expansion of our military strength. That expansion had not been proceeding as far as we had hoped. The best of all we had to give had gone to the British Expeditionary Force, and although they had not the numbers of tanks and some articles of equipment which were desirable, they were a very well and finely equipped army. They had the first fruits of all that our industry had to give, and that is gone. And now here is this further delay. How long it will be, how long it will last, depends upon the exertions which we make in this island. An effort, the like of which has never been seen in our records, is now being made. Work is proceeding everywhere, night and day, Sundays and week days. Capital and labour have cast aside their interests, rights, and customs and put them into the common stock. Already the flow of munitions has leaped forward. There is no reason why we should not in a few months overtake the sudden and serious loss that has come upon us, without retarding the development of our general programme.

Nevertheless, our thankfulness at the escape of our army and so many men, whose loved ones have passed through an agonising week, must not blind us to the fact that what has happened in France and Belgium is a colossal military disaster. The French army has been weakened, the Belgian army has been lost, a large part of those fortified lines upon which so much faith had been reposed is gone, many valuable mining districts and factories have passed into the enemy's possession, the whole of the Channel ports are in his hands, with all the tragic consequences that follow from that, and we must expect another blow to be struck almost immediately at us or at France. We are told that Herr Hitler has a plan for invading the British Isles. This has often been thought of before. When Napoleon lay at Boulogne for a year with his flat-bottomed boats and his Grand Army, he was told by someone, 'There are bitter weeds in England.' There are certainly a great many more of them since the British Expeditionary Force returned.

The whole question of home defence against invasion is, of course, powerfully affected by the fact that we have for the time being in this island incomparably more powerful military forces than we have ever had at any moment in this war or the last. But this will not continue. We shall not be content with a defensive war. We have our duty to our ally. We have to reconstitute and build up the British Expeditionary Force once again, under its gallant Commander-in-Chief, Lord Gort. All this is in train; but in the interval we must put our defences in this island into such a high state of organisation that the fewest possible numbers will be required to give effective security and that the largest possible potential of offensive effort may be realised. On this we are now engaged. It will be very convenient, if it be the desire of the House, to enter upon this subject in a secret session. Not that the government would necessarily be able to reveal in very great detail military secrets, but we like to have our discussions free, without the restraint imposed by the fact that they will be read the next day by the enemy; and the government would benefit by views freely expressed in all parts of the House by members with their knowledge of so many different parts of the country. I understand that some request is to be made upon this subject, which will be readily acceded to by His Majesty's government.

We have found it necessary to take measures of increasing stringency, not only against enemy aliens and suspicious characters of other nationalities, but also against British subjects who may become a danger or a nuisance should the war be transported to the United Kingdom. I know there are a great many people affected by the orders which we have made who are the passionate enemies of Nazi Germany. I am very sorry for them, but we cannot, at the present time and under the present stress, draw all the distinctions which we should like to do. If parachute landings were attempted and fierce fighting attendant upon them followed, these unfortunate people would be far better out of the way, for their own sakes as well as for ours. There is, however, another class, for which I feel not the slightest sympathy. Parliament has given us the powers to put down fifth column activities with a strong hand, and we shall use those powers subject to the supervision and correction of the House, without the slightest hesitation until we are satisfied, and more than satisfied, that this malignancy in our midst has been effectively stamped out.

Turning once again, and this time more generally, to the question of invasion, I would observe that there has never been a period in all these long centuries of which we boast when an absolute guarantee against invasion, still less against serious raids, could have been given to our people. In the days of Napoleon the same wind which would have carried his transports across the Channel might have driven away the blockading fleet. There was always the chance, and it is that chance which has excited and befooled the imaginations of many continental tyrants. Many are the tales that are told. We are assured that novel methods will be adopted, and when we see the originality of malice, the ingenuity of aggression, which our enemy displays, we may certainly prepare ourselves for every kind of novel stratagem and every kind of brutal and treacherous manoeuvre. I think that no idea is so outlandish that it should not be considered and viewed with a searching, but at the same time, I hope, with a steady eye. We must never forget the solid assurances of sea power and those which belong to air power if it can be locally exercised.

I have, myself, full confidence that if all do their duty, if nothing is neglected, and if the best arrangements are made, as they are being made, we shall prove ourselves once again able to defend our island home, to ride out the storm of war, and to outlive the menace of tyranny, if necessary for years, if necessary alone. At any rate, that is what we are going to try to do. That is the resolve of His Majesty's government – every man of them. That is the will of parliament and the nation. The British Empire and the French Republic, linked together in their cause and in their need, will defend to the death their native soil, aiding each other like good comrades to the utmost of their strength. Even though large tracts of Europe and many old and famous states have fallen or may fall into the grip of the Gestapo and all the odious apparatus of Nazi rule, we shall not flag or fail.

We shall go on to the end, we shall fight in France, we shall fight on the seas and oceans, we shall fight with growing confidence and growing strength in the air, we shall defend our island, whatever the cost may be, we shall fight on the beaches, we shall fight on the landing grounds, we shall fight in the fields and in the streets, we shall fight in the hills; we shall never surrender, and even if, which I do not for a moment believe, this island or a large part of it were subjugated and starving, then our empire beyond the seas, armed and guarded by the British fleet, would carry on the struggle, until, in God's good time, the new world, with all its power and might, steps forth to the rescue and the liberation of the old.

Speech © Winston S Churchill.
Reproduced with permission of Curtis Brown Ltd, London
on behalf of The Estate of Winston Churchill.

This report of Churchill's address to parliament appeared
in the *Manchester Guardian* on June 5 1940.

PREMIER FACES THE ISSUES
From our political correspondent

Westminster, Tuesday

The House of Commons, at the time of writing, is still trying
to adjust itself to one of the gravest speeches ever made to it
in all its long history. It shattered any illusions that the withdrawal of the BEF and the French troops from Northern
France has turned a military defeat into a victory. 'A miracle
of deliverance' – that it was, Mr Churchill agreed, won by discipline, resource, skill, and unconquerable fidelity. But let no one,
was his warning, assign any attributes of victory to what
happened. Wars were not won by evacuations. And then one
heard Mr Churchill, with the House hanging on every syllable,
saying with remorseless candour that was clearly bent on sparing
us nothing of the truth: 'No; this is a colossal military disaster.'

The proof? Mr Churchill provided it. The French army
had been weakened, the Belgian army had been lost, part
of the allied fortified line had gone, valuable mining districts
had passed into the enemy's possession, the whole of the
Channel ports were in his hands, and we had abandoned an
enormous quantity of material, including a thousand guns.

Facing the possibilities

The House was certainly getting the picture presented to it in a true and grim perspective. 'Hug no more delusions,' Mr Churchill seemed to be saying. For he had not finished. He squared up to all foreseeable developments and examined each fearlessly with the House following him in deepening gravity. There was a possibility that Hitler might strike at France or he might strike at us. He discussed a German invasion rather as a probability than a possibility. Finally, he confronted the disastrous contingency (though, he said, he could not for a moment believe in it as an actuality) – the possibility of the subjugation of a great part of these islands. But if that moment came the war would still not be over. Our empire, guarded by the British fleet, would then take up the struggle until the new world was ushered in. After this, surely no one is going to accuse Mr Churchill or his government of complacency.

Deliverance

Of course, there was a bright side. No one who reads Mr Churchill will complain that he underrates the allies' withdrawal from Dunkirk either as a feat of arms or as an immortal example of heroism. Nor should his glowing passage about the RAF be overlooked, with its moving tribute to these young men (his voice seemed to falter a little with emotion) who made the Crusaders and the Knights of the Round Table look not only remote but prosaic. But that was not all on the credit side. Mr Churchill found a victory at the heart of the miraculous deliverance, the victory of these young men over the German air force, for this, said Mr Churchill, had been a great trial of strength between the two opposing air forces, and the enemy had been forced to pay fourfold for every loss he had inflicted upon the RAF. We might feel greatly reassured by these facts, Mr Churchill thought, when we came to consider the prospects of aerial attack on this country.

But for all this drastic realism, Mr Churchill did not doubt for one moment that if we all did our part (and the nation was now putting forth an unprecedented effort) we should safely ride out the storms. The attitude of the House was worthy of all praise. As Mr Churchill gradually unfolded the position, its spirits rose instead of drooped, and in the end there was a long and defiant cheer underlining Mr Churchill's closing declaration that, if need were, we would fight in France, on the sea, in the air, on the beaches, on the landing-grounds, in the fields, in the streets, and in the hills, and we would never surrender. And, of course, there was great cheering when Mr Churchill disclosed the amazing number of the men brought back from Dunkirk – 335,000 or 305,000 more than Mr Churchill deemed possible last week. It was not without a pang that the House heard from Mr Churchill that we had lost 30,000 killed, wounded, and missing.

The flame of
French resistance

CHARLES DE GAULLE
June 18, 19, 22 1940

These speeches were delivered by
Charles de Gaulle and broadcast by the BBC
on June 18, 19 and 22 1940.

FOREWORD

Antony Beevor

Antony Beevor is a military historian and the author of *Stalingrad, Berlin: The Downfall 1945*, and co-author of *Paris after the Liberation 1944–1949*.

Charles de Gaulle was only 15 when he first revealed his dream to lead the armies of France and save its honour. A strong sense of history was matched by a love of the French language, and his mesmerising oratory later helped the junior general of 1940 to become the political leader who towered over his country's destiny.

The German invasion of France, which began in May 1940, proved devastating. General de Gaulle's 4th Armoured Division, advancing bravely into battle near Laon on May 17, was decimated by Stukas and forced to withdraw. After another more successful attack, he was summoned at the end of the month to Paris, where he saw Paul Reynaud, the prime minister. Reynaud offered him a junior post in the government, but he had also invited Marshal Philippe Pétain, the hero of Verdun, to join the cabinet as vice-president. And Pétain led the faction of *capitulards* who wanted to come to terms with the Nazis. De Gaulle, formerly the most favoured disciple of the old marshal, had now fallen out with him.

Paris was abandoned on June 10. Amid chaos and demoralisation, the government retreated along roads swarming with refugees all the way to Bordeaux. On June 16, Reynaud was outmanoeuvred at the council of ministers and resigned. De Gaulle, who had been with Churchill in London, flew back to Bordeaux that night and heard that Pétain would seek an armistice. He too was now in the wilderness and at risk of arrest for wanting to fight on. He went to see Reynaud, who in spite of his resignation, provided him with passports and money.

Early next morning, June 17, de Gaulle fled France in a biplane with Churchill's representative, General Edward Spears. To fly over the English Channel was akin to crossing the Rubicon. De Gaulle was now technically a rebel and a deserter from the army he loved. The turbulence of his feelings can never be in doubt. Years later, when the writer and statesman André Malraux asked him about this moment, he took both of Malraux's hands in his. 'Oh, Malraux,' he said slowly. 'It was frightful.'

They landed at Heston aerodrome soon after midday, unaware that Marshal Pétain was announcing the armistice to the French nation at that moment. For the majority of his listeners, refugees and demoralised soldiers alike, this was what they desperately wanted to hear. The fact that it was Pétain, with his reputation as a great military hero, who had stopped the fighting cleansed them of guilt. The new father of the nation had assumed their responsibilities.

Spears took de Gaulle and Courcel to see Churchill in the garden at Downing Street. There, in the afternoon sunshine, as de Gaulle's biographer, Jean Lacouture, describes, the tall, awkward Frenchman asked for help in 'hoisting the colours'. He wanted to use the BBC to address the French people. Churchill agreed without hesitation. De Gaulle set to work that evening to draft his speech, chain-smoking as always.

The next morning, several members of the war cabinet were uneasy about the speech. Their chief priority was to persuade the government in Bordeaux to refuse to hand over the French fleet to the Germans. De Gaulle's proclamation of revolt from London might well prove counter-productive at such a moment. But after further discussion round the table, agreement was reached. Duff Cooper, the minister of information, gave de Gaulle lunch, and then left him to finish correcting his text.

De Gaulle and his aide took a taxi to Broadcasting House, where they were conducted to Studio 4B. The General was asked to say something to check the voice level. 'La France', he intoned in his deep voice. One of those present described how pale he was and that his brown forelock was glued to his forehead. 'He stared at the microphone as though it were

France and as though he wanted to hypnotise it. His voice was clear, firm and rather loud, the voice of a man speaking to his troops before battle. He did not seem nervous, but extremely tense, as though he were concentrating all his power in one single moment.'

De Gaulle does not launch into a diatribe against Pétain and the other *capitulards* who were soon to become the men of Vichy. He simply starts with the bare facts, but using the odd loaded word, such as when he says: 'Alleging the defeat of our armies, this government has entered into negotiations with the enemy.' While this very brief address becomes rich in the rhetoric of defiance, it also proves extraordinarily prophetic. The battle of France may have been lost, he says, but France was not alone, and she and Britain would be able to 'draw unreservedly on the immense industrial resources of the United States'. France may have been 'crushed by the sheer weight of mechanised force' hurled against it, 'but we can still look to a future in which even greater mechanised force will bring us victory. The destiny of the world is at stake.' He then finishes with his personal appeal, calling on all French officers and men who can to rally to him, and promises to speak again. His language, using the wavelike repetitions of classical oratory, acts like a poetic drumroll.

De Gaulle's address of June 19 is even shorter. He claims that the French state has collapsed, 'that all ordinary forms of authority have disappeared'. The 'disintegration of a government in thrall to the enemy' prompted him now to 'speak for France', and call upon soldiers and sailors in North Africa and elsewhere to resist the invaders and rally to his cause.

The longest of the three speeches was made on June 22. Now that Pétain's acceptance of the humiliating terms was starting to emerge, de Gaulle feels free to speak out far more strongly. The armistice would reduce France to slavery. His own determination to fight on now implicitly puts him and his handful of followers on a par with the governments-in-exile of other occupied countries, such as Poland, Norway, Holland, Belgium and Luxembourg. Once again he re-emphasises that this was not just a war between Germany and France. It was a world war and the industrial might of the United States would eventually prevail. He calls again upon all soldiers to join him and asks their commanders to contact him.

Few may have heard the original speech of June 18, but it was reproduced, at least in part, in several French provincial newspapers and word spread. But back in London, de Gaulle's hosts soon found how prickly and difficult he could be. The BBC was rather taken aback when he announced over the air without warning them that he would be speaking again the following night. The Foreign Office was horrified by the more direct attacks on the Bordeaux government in the second speech and complained to Churchill. The future of the French navy still perturbed them.

De Gaulle, proud, unbending and infinitely touchy, would soon provoke his hosts, especially Churchill, to rage against his obstinacy and ingratitude. But that speech of June 18, although delivered on the inconvenient anniversary of the battle of Waterloo, was the rallying call to a defeated France. It became the moment to which France could look with pride over the following difficult years, and bind the otherwise mortal wounds of humiliation with the great myth of the liberation which de Gaulle himself proclaimed from the Hôtel de Ville in Paris on 25 August, 1944. 'Paris outraged, Paris broken, Paris martyred, but Paris liberated! Liberated by herself, liberated by her people, with the help of the whole of France, that is to say of fighting France, the true France, eternal France.' There was no acknowledgment of the British, who had given him shelter, nor of the Americans whose 'immense industrial resources' had made the victory possible, as he had so accurately predicted. His obsessive national pride would not allow it.

The flame of
French resistance

CHARLES DE GAULLE
June 18, 19, 22 1940

June 18 1940

The leaders who, for many years past, have been at the head of the French armed forces have set up a government.

Alleging the defeat of our armies, this government has entered into negotiations with the enemy with a view to bringing about a cessation of hostilities.

It is quite true that we were, and still are, overwhelmed by enemy mechanised forces, both on the ground and in the air. It was the tanks, the planes, and the tactics of the Germans, far more than the fact that we were outnumbered, that forced our armies to retreat. It was the German tanks, planes, and tactics that provided the element of surprise which brought our leaders to their present plight.

But has the last word been said? Must we abandon all hope? Is our defeat final and irremediable? To those questions I answer – No!

Speaking in full knowledge of the facts, I ask you to

believe me when I say that the cause of France is not lost. The very factors that brought about our defeat may one day lead us to victory.

For, remember this, France does not stand alone. She is not isolated. Behind her is a vast empire, and she can make common cause with the British empire, which commands the seas and is continuing the struggle. Like England, she can draw unreservedly on the immense industrial resources of the United States.

This war is not limited to our unfortunate country. The outcome of the struggle has not been decided by the battle of France. This is a world war. Mistakes have been made, there have been delays and untold suffering, but the fact remains that there still exists in the world everything we need to crush our enemies some day.

Today we are crushed by the sheer weight of mechanised force hurled against us, but we can still look to a future in which even greater mechanised force will bring us victory. The destiny of the world is at stake.

I, General de Gaulle, now in London, call on all French officers and men who are at present on British soil, or may be in the future, with or without their arms; I call on all engineers and skilled workmen from the armaments factories who are at present on British soil, or may be in the future, to get in touch with me.

Whatever happens, the flame of French resistance must not and shall not die.

Tomorrow I shall broadcast again from London.

June 19 1940

Frenchmen must now be fully aware that all ordinary forms of authority have disappeared.

Faced by the bewilderment of my countrymen, by the disintegration of a government in thrall to the enemy, by the fact that the institutions of my country are incapable, at the moment, of functioning, I, General de Gaulle, a French soldier and military leader, realise that I now speak for France.

In the name of France, I make the following solemn declaration: It is the bounden duty of all Frenchmen who still bear arms to continue the struggle. For them to lay down their arms, to evacuate any position of military importance, or agree to hand over any part of French territory, however small, to enemy control, would be a crime against our country. For the moment I refer particularly to French North Africa – to the integrity of French North Africa.

The Italian armistice is nothing but a clumsy trap. In the Africa of Clauzel, Bugeaud, Lyautey, and Noguès, honour and duty strictly enjoin that the French should refuse to carry out the conditions imposed by the enemy.

The thought that the panic of Bordeaux could make itself felt across the sea is not to be borne.

Soldiers of France, wherever you may be, arise!

June 22 1940

The French government, after having asked for an armistice, now knows the conditions dictated by the enemy.

The result of these conditions would be the complete demobilisation of the French land, sea, and air forces, the surrender of our weapons and the total occupation of French territory. The French government would come under German and Italian tutelage.

It may therefore be said that this armistice would not only be a capitulation, but that it would also reduce the country to slavery. Now, a great many Frenchmen refuse to accept either capitulation or slavery, for reasons which are called: honour, common sense, and the higher interests of the country.

I say honour, for France has undertaken not to lay down arms save in agreement with her allies. As long as the allies continue the war, her government has no right to surrender to the enemy. The Polish, Norwegian, Belgian, Netherlands, and Luxemburg governments, though driven from their territories, have thus interpreted their duty.

I say common sense, for it is absurd to consider the struggle as lost. True, we have suffered a major defeat. We lost the battle of France through a faulty military system, mistakes in the conduct of operations, and the defeatist spirit shown by the government during recent battles. But we still have a vast empire, our fleet is intact, and we possess large sums in gold. We still have the gigantic potentialities of American industry. The same war conditions which caused us to be beaten by 5,000 planes and 6,000 tanks can tomorrow bring victory by means of 20,000 tanks and 20,000 planes.

I say the higher interests of the country, for this is not a Franco-German war to be decided by a single battle. This is a world war. No one can foresee whether the neutral countries of today will not be at war tomorrow, or whether Germany's allies will always remain her allies. If the powers of freedom ultimately triumph over those of servitude, what will be the fate of a France which has submitted to the enemy?

Honour, common sense, and the interests of the country require that all free Frenchmen, wherever they be, should continue the fight as best they may.

It is therefore necessary to group the largest possible French force wherever this can be done. Everything which can be collected by way of French military elements and potentialities for armaments production must be organised wherever such elements exist.

I, General de Gaulle, am undertaking this national task here in England.

I call upon all French servicemen of the land, sea, and air forces; I call upon French engineers and skilled armaments workers who are on British soil, or have the means of getting here, to come and join me.

I call upon the leaders, together with all soldiers, sailors, and airmen of the French land, sea, and air forces, wherever they may now be, to get in touch with me.

I call upon all Frenchmen who want to remain free to listen to my voice and follow me.

Long live free France in honour and independence!

The *Manchester Guardian* published the first two reports below after de Gaulle's initial broadcasts; the third, which ran after the liberation of Paris, suggests the broadcasts helped establish him as a national leader. The second two reports have been abridged.

'FIGHT ON HERE'

A French general's appeal

June 19 1940

An appeal to French soldiers, engineers and skilled workmen who have reached British soil to get in touch with him so as to continue the fight was broadcast from London last night by General de Gaulle, Under Secretary to the Ministry of National Defence in the Reynaud Government.

He said: 'We certainly have been and still are submerged by the mechanical strength of the enemy, both on land and in the air. The tanks, the aeroplanes, the tactics of the Germans far more than their numbers were responsible for our retirement and surprised our generals to such an extent that they have been brought to the position which they are in today.

'France is not lost. The same methods which have brought about our defeat can quite well one day bring victory. Whatever happens the flame of French resistance must not and shall not be extinguished.'

Organising resistance June 25 1940

'I have reason to believe that the French fleet will not surrender,' said General de Gaulle to a reporter in London yesterday when asked if he had received any promise of support for allies from the French fleet.

General de Gaulle on Saturday [June 22] broadcast from London a message to the French people, and on Sunday, after the armistice terms had been announced, he appealed to French people in Britain and his countrymen in France and in the French empire to rally round him and the French National Committee which was being formed in London to continue the struggle against aggression.

Dismissed

It has been reported that because of these broadcasts, the French government in Bordeaux has dismissed General de Gaulle from the French army and ordered him to be court-martialled. Questioned about this he said: 'I have had no official communication of Marshal Petain's decision. Whatever happens it will not change my position.'

The general revealed that he was in communication with General Noguès, Commander of French forces in Morocco and with General Catoux, who is in charge of French forces in Indo-China. 'From the information I have received,' said the general, 'I am convinced that all parts of the empire will go on fighting.'

Quick response

General de Gaulle said he had received an almost un-believable response from French residents in Britain to his broadcast. He had also received messages from people still living in France and from the whole French empire. He displayed a pile of telegrams, among them messages from Tangiers, Damascus and New York. The General was asked if, apart from in the French Empire, it was intended to organise resistance in France itself. He replied that France would be thoroughly occupied but that 'at the first military success we have, it will be possible to organise some kind of resistance on French soil'. General de Gaulle has opened offices in Stephen's House, Victoria Embankment, London.

The Fourth Republic, Tuesday August 29 1944

The wave of national enthusiasm which has lifted General de Gaulle to the head of France and placed him in liber-ated Paris will inevitably recede, to be followed by that calm which comes after, as well as before, the storm. The man who has thus been raised to the summit of his ambition will be faced with opportunities and responsibilities such as are rarely given by history. What will he do with them?

Rarely has a leader been at once so famous and so little known to his people. To the French he is first and foremost the man who proclaimed his faith in resistance when other and better-known leaders had failed; since then he has been presented to the French people by all the enormous power of the BBC and the allied propaganda machine as the virile leader of the new France. And how well he has sustained the part! The great events of the past days have been sufficient proof of his achievements.

of the 1990s, and the above probability matrix to the
implied residuals the new figures. And here will be the
absolute worth the great cost of the past very few
hectic afternoons of a few solemn faces.

A tryst with destiny

JAWAHARLAL NEHRU
August 14 1947

This speech was delivered by Jawaharlal Nehru
to the Constituent Assembly of India in New Delhi
on August 14 1947.

Ian Jack

Ian Jack worked as correspondent in India from 1977 to 1988. He is now a writer and has been the editor of *Granta* since 1995.

The demand for Indian independence had small beginnings in the early 20th century, but by the 1920s it loomed large in Indian life and British politics: demonstrations, hunger strikes, imprisonments, round-table conferences, Gandhi meeting the King. A slow dance of two steps forward and one back; but when the great day came, it came with astonishing speed.

By the 1940s, British politicians, apart from Churchill, realised independence would soon be inevitable, though none knew if India would become one nation or two, with a separate Muslim homeland under the recently coined name, Pakistan. Plans for a single federal nation attracted insufficient support in 1946. The Labour government then appointed a new viceroy, Louis Mountbatten, under orders to get Britain out by June 1948. Mountbatten did better than that. He arrived in Delhi on March 22 1947, and India (and Pakistan) declared independence less than five months later.

Whether such speed was wise has been debated ever since: a better-organised withdrawal might have saved hundreds of thousands of lives, but might merely have postponed the carnage. The partition of India prompted the largest migration in human history – up to 15 million left their homes, something that was never likely to happen bloodlessly. More certainly, it was the personalities of two men – Mountbatten and Jawaharlal Nehru – that enabled independence to be achieved so quickly. The adjectives 'dashing', 'charming' and 'mercurial' may cover many flaws but they applied to India's last viceroy and its first prime minister. They made a handsome spectacle of friendship (which the founders of Pakistan interpreted as alliance and never forgot or forgave).

Independence day was set for August 15. Then the astrologers said August 14 was the more auspicious date. Nehru compromised. India's assembly would be convened on the afternoon of August 14 and continue in session until Nehru's speech shortly before midnight, when, to the chiming of an English clock and the blowing of Indian conch shells, independent India would be born. Dressed in a golden silk jacket with a red rose in the buttonhole, Nehru rose to speak. His sentences were finely made and memorable – Nehru was a good writer; his *Discovery of India* stands well above the level reached by most politician-writers.

Nehru was then 57 and widowed after what had been an unhappy arranged marriage. He spoke in the language that came naturally to him, an English acquired through Harrow, Cambridge, the Inner Temple. There were poetic, Edwardian touches – the 'tryst with destiny', the 'midnight hour' – and the odd poetic licence: 'the world sleeps' hardly applied to Britain, where it was early evening, or America, which was having lunch.

Some footnotes are in order. When Nehru says the pledge for freedom will be redeemed 'not wholly or in full measure' he is referring to partition. When he refers to 'the greatest man of our generation . . . the architect of this freedom, the father of our nation' he means Gandhi. When he mentions the pains that 'continue even now' he has in mind the slaughter between Hindus and Muslims that began the previous year and which was becoming crueller and bloodier. As Nehru spoke he was aware that Sir Cyril Radcliffe had delivered the report that would clumsily define the new boundaries of India and Pakistan and split the Sikh Punjab into two. Mountbatten insisted it was kept quiet until after August 15.

Gandhi was not in the chamber to hear Nehru's speech but in Calcutta, doing his best to quell Muslim-Hindu riots. He and Nehru had, at least politically, a father-son relationship but their mutual feelings had cooled. Gandhi opposed partition and had instead suggested that a Muslim be made prime minister of an undivided India. Nehru, frustrated by Gandhi's incessant moralising, thought that he was out of touch with pressing reality. Even so, he made his most heartfelt speech (though it never became as famous as this one) when Gandhi was assassinated five months later. Given the horrendous surrounding events, it would be easy to see Nehru's rhetoric as that of a desperate man whistling in the dark. But it wasn't seen that way then, nor should it be now. The nobility of Nehru's words – their sheer sweep – provided the new India with a lodestone that was ambitious and humane. Post-colonialism began here as well as Indian democracy, which has since outlived many expectations of its death. When Nehru spoke, there were approximately 250 million citizens of India. Sixty years later, there are four times as many.

A tryst with destiny

JAWAHARLAL NEHRU
August 14 1947

Long years ago we made a tryst with destiny, and now the time comes when we shall redeem our pledge, not wholly or in full measure, but very substantially.

At the stroke of the midnight hour, when the world sleeps, India will awake to life and freedom. A moment comes, which comes but rarely in history, when we step out from the old to the new, when an age ends, and when the soul of a nation, long suppressed, finds utterance.

It is fitting that at this solemn moment we take the pledge of dedication to the service of India and her people and to the still larger cause of humanity.

At the dawn of history India started on her unending quest, and trackless centuries are filled with her striving and the grandeur of her success and her failures. Through good and ill fortune alike she has never lost sight of that quest or forgotten the ideals which gave her strength. We end today a period of ill fortune and India discovers herself again.

The achievement we celebrate today is but a step, an opening of opportunity, to the greater triumphs and achievements that await us. Are we brave enough and wise enough to grasp this opportunity and accept the challenge of the future?

Freedom and power bring responsibility. The responsibility rests upon this assembly, a sovereign body representing the sovereign people of India. Before the birth of freedom we have endured all the pains of labour and our hearts are heavy with the memory of this sorrow. Some of those pains continue even now. Nevertheless, the past is over and it is the future that beckons to us now.

That future is not one of ease or resting but of incessant striving so that we may fulfil the pledges we have so often taken and the one we shall take today. The service of India means the service of the millions who suffer. It means the ending of poverty and ignorance and disease and inequality of opportunity.

The ambition of the greatest man of our generation has been to wipe every tear from every eye. That may be beyond us, but as long as there are tears and suffering, so long our work will not be over.

And so we have to labour and to work, and work hard, to give reality to our dreams. Those dreams are for India, but they are also for the world, for all the nations and peoples are too closely knit together today for any one of them to imagine that it can live apart.

Peace has been said to be indivisible; so is freedom, so is

prosperity now, and so also is disaster in this one world that can no longer be split into isolated fragments.

To the people of India, whose representatives we are, we make an appeal to join us with faith and confidence in this great adventure. This is no time for petty and destructive criticism, no time for ill will or blaming others. We have to build the noble mansion of free India where all her children may dwell.

The appointed day has come – the day appointed by destiny – and India stands forth again, after long slumber and struggle, awake, vital, free and independent. The past clings on to us still in some measure and we have to do much before we redeem the pledges we have so often taken. Yet the turning point is past, and history begins anew for us, the history which we shall live and act and others will write about.

It is a fateful moment for us in India, for all Asia and for the world. A new star rises, the star of freedom in the east, a new hope comes into being, a vision long cherished materialises. May the star never set and that hope never be betrayed!

We rejoice in that freedom, even though clouds surround us, and many of our people are sorrow-stricken and difficult problems encompass us. But freedom brings responsibilities and burdens and we have to face them in the spirit of a free and disciplined people.

On this day our first thoughts go to the architect of this freedom, the father of our nation, who, embodying the old spirit of India, held aloft the torch of freedom and lighted up the darkness that surrounded us.

We have often been unworthy followers of his and have strayed from his message, but not only we but succeeding generations will remember this message and bear the imprint in their hearts of this great son of India, magnificent in his faith and strength and courage and humility. We shall never allow that torch of freedom to be blown out, however high the wind or stormy the tempest.

Our next thoughts must be of the unknown volunteers and soldiers of freedom who, without praise or reward, have served India even unto death.

We think also of our brothers and sisters who have been cut off from us by political boundaries and who unhappily cannot share at present in the freedom that has come. They are of us and will remain of us whatever may happen, and we shall be sharers in their good and ill fortune alike.

The future beckons to us. Whither do we go and what shall be our endeavour? To bring freedom and opportunity to the common man, to the peasants and workers of India; to fight and end poverty and ignorance and disease; to build up a prosperous, democratic and progressive nation, and to create social, economic and political institutions which will ensure justice and fullness of life to every man and woman.

We have hard work ahead. There is no resting for any one of us till we redeem our pledge in full, till we make all the people of India what destiny intended them to be.

We are citizens of a great country, on the verge of bold

advance, and we have to live up to that high standard. All of us, to whatever religion we may belong, are equally the children of India with equal rights, privileges and obligations. We cannot encourage communalism or narrow-mindedness, for no nation can be great whose people are narrow in thought or in action.

To the nations and peoples of the world we send greetings and pledge ourselves to cooperate with them in furthering peace, freedom and democracy.

And to India, our much-loved motherland, the ancient, the eternal and the ever-new, we pay our reverent homage and we bind ourselves afresh to her service. Jai Hind [Victory to India].

The following articles ran in the *Manchester Guardian*
on August 15 1947 as India became independent.
Some have been abridged.

DELHI REJOICES AND MR GANDHI FASTS
India wakes to life and freedom

The Indian Constituent Assembly met at midnight last night
in New Delhi for its 'independence meeting'.

Over two thousand members of the Assembly sat in the
beflagged hall under the dazzle of arc lights. To a hushed
house Mr Nehru, now Premier of India, said: 'Long years ago
we made a tryst with destiny and now the time comes when
we shall redeem our pledge not wholly or in full measure, but
substantially. At the stroke of midnight, the hour when the
world sleeps, India will wake to life and freedom. We end
today a period of ill-fortune and India discovers herself again.

'The ambition of Mr Gandhi, the greatest man of our
generation, has been to wipe every tear from every eye. That
may be beyond us, but so long as there are tears and suffering
our work will not be over.'

At the end of the meeting Mr Nehru and Mr Prasad,
President of the Assembly, left to inform Lord Mountbatten
that his appointment as Governor General had been
endorsed.

Celebrations

Outside the Assembly, the city was celebrating with guns, temple bells, fireworks, parades, and rejoicing in the streets, which included the burning of an effigy of British imperialism. Three hundred flag-raising ceremonies had been arranged throughout the Dominion. All Hindu temples and Muslim mosques remained open for prayers. In Bombay, sirens of hundreds of mills and factories, the whistling of railway engines, and hooting from ships ushered in independence at midnight. – *Reuter and Associated Press*

Calcutta's wildly happy scenes: Mr Gandhi starts fast

From our special correspondent

Hindus and Muslims, freely mixing with each other, are in Calcutta tonight wildly celebrating the approach of independence. The former scenes of communal battles are now happy meeting places for crowds of both communities who are shouting and dancing in the streets. No incident has been reported until a late hour tonight. Mr Gandhi, Mr Suhrawardhy, who ceases to be the Premier of Bengal at midnight, and a former mayor of Calcutta are beginning a 24-hour fast to celebrate independence.

Farewell and hail birth of two dominions:
India and Pakistan celebrate

British rule in India ended at midnight last night, after 163 years. Today the new Dominions of India and Pakistan are in being.

At midnight in Delhi, capital of India, Lord Mountbatten ceased to be the Viceroy and became the Governor General of India. It is announced in London that an earldom has been conferred on him. At midnight in Karachi, capital of Pakistan, Mr Jinnah became Governor General of Pakistan.

The Pakistan Constituent Assembly met yesterday afternoon and Lord Mountbatten was there to say farewell: not an absolute parting, he said, but a parting among friends. The Indian Constituent Assembly held an 'independence meeting' at midnight: the hour, said Mr Nehru, the Indian Premier, 'when the world sleeps' and India wakes 'to life and freedom'.

The US announced yesterday that it is giving full diplomatic recognition to Pakistan. China is doing the same, and Egypt is to establish diplomatic relations with India and Pakistan.

Indian independence – leading article

The British people have no yearly celebration of a national birthday, for it would be hard to say when the life of contemporary Britain began, but in this respect they are unusual. To many countries a national day is as necessary as a national flag. July 4 and July 14 are likely to be hallowed for centuries, and October 10 to be revered by many hundred million Chinese of the future. Today, August 15, on which Indian independence is inaugurated, may in time become a date no less revered than these other anniversaries, and by an even larger number of people.

And the Indian national day may also have a prouder distinction. For while the national days of other countries so often commemorate glorious but bloody events Indians today are able to rejoice at achieving their independence without the prelude of country-wide civil war to which some months ago many had resigned themselves.

On such a day, the mind will turn first to the men whose work has made it possible. Nehru, Jinnah and above all Gandhi, will loom as figures larger than life. Those who have taken a part in the recent affairs, however humble, may well say:

How many ages hence
Shall this our lofty scene be acted o'er
In States unborn and accents yet unknown!
. . . So oft as that shall be
So often shall the knot of us be called
The men that gave their country liberty

A sorrowful shadow

Today's celebration is a time for gladness in India – marred though it must be by the shadow of famine over so much of the country, and by the rioting in Calcutta and the Punjab – and for dedication to service in the future. The atmosphere, if still electric, is rather that which follows than that which precedes a storm.

But Indians have not fought for independence in the belief that it was a bed of roses. They have claimed, naturally and rightly, the honour of confronting and fighting the

dangers with which their country is faced and of freely
invoking or dispensing with the aid which may be offered
them from outside. It is a resolution which every man of
spirit will applaud. Today, however, is not the time for
thinking too much of dangers.

The end of an empire

For Indians, it is thus a time to look both forwards and
backwards, and an Englishman also may be inclined to see
present events not only as a new start but as arising out of
and the culmination of the century and a half of the British
connection. He will review the strange history of the
British Empire in India.

As has so often been pointed out, the British went to
India not to conquer but to trade. Events, not intention,
created the British Raj. The wheel has come full circle and
the British who went to India to trade are now once more
in India only as traders. But traders have their part to play
in society; and behind the traders lies, if India desires to
invoke it and ally itself with it, the organised and co-operating
strength not only of the British nation but of the British
Commonwealth. But whether India desires such co-operation,
that is for India, not this country, to decide. The British Raj
is dead.

The two flags – London

An order given in Aldwych this morning was the signal for
proud contingents of Indian soldiers and airmen to come

to attention and for thousands of people to look skywards. The Union Jack was already flying from India House with what appeared to be a bare flagpole beside it. Then Mr Vellodi, the acting High Commissioner for India, jerked at a rope and the flag of the new Dominion of India fluttered into view – saffron, white and green, and with the blue spinning wheel of Asoka in the centre. Above cheering, loudspeakers carried the voices of women in India House who were singing *Bow to the Motherland*, and here and there among the crowd were heard shouts of 'Jai Hind!' ('Victory to India!').

The simple ceremony had followed another inside India House where Mr Ebrahim Rahimtoola, the High Commissioner for Pakistan, sat beside Mr Krishna Menon, the new High Commissioner for India. But for many the unfurling of the flag was the symbol of independence.

Some of the spectators at India House made their way later to Lancaster House, where they crowded the red-carpeted hall, stairs and gallery for the Pakistan ceremony. The new High Commissioner, Mr Rahimtoola, described the hoisting of the Pakistan flag as symbolic 'not only of an ideal achieved but also of the tremendous task which lies ahead'.

An Indian observer, who was at the India House ceremony, noted politely that 'it was a day of Indian summer'. The flag was clearly seen. He explained that the colours represented courage, sacrifice and trust – 'the principles upon which Mahatma Gandhi has sought to guide India's struggle for independence'.

The cult of the individual

NIKITA KHRUSHCHEV
February 25 1956

This is an edited version of a speech delivered by
Nikita Khrushchev to the 20th Congress of the Communist
party of the USSR in Moscow on February 25 1956.

For ease of reading, individual excisions are not marked,
nor is it indicated when the case of a letter changes
due to the deletion of part of a sentence.

Mikhail Gorbachev

Mikhail Gorbachev was the reforming
leader of the USSR 1985–1991.

The 20th Congress of the Communist party holds a unique
place in Soviet history, due to Nikita Khrushchev's report
On the Cult of the Individual. The speech was prepared
in strict secrecy, and Khrushchev kept working on it during
the Congress. He gave the speech on February 25 1956 at
a closed meeting, after the new party leadership was elected.
The speech shocked delegates, all committed communists,
and then wider Soviet society. It accused Joseph Stalin of
creating a personality cult. It debunked the myth of Stalin
as 'the disciple of Lenin': in fact, under the guise of fighting
the 'enemies of the people' Stalin had eliminated Lenin's
closest associates.

Khrushchev cited facts about Joseph Stalin's criminal

deeds, of which the people knew little or nothing. For the first time, he spoke not only about the murder of Sergei Kirov and the execution of delegates to the 17th party Congress, but also about the abuse of prisoners. Stalin, who had been venerated as next to God, was revealed as the instigator of mass repression. Despite the damning revelations, the speech's overall assessment of Stalin was relatively mild. In this, Khrushchev yielded to the pressure of conservatives like Molotov. He said, for example, that 'in the past Stalin undoubtedly performed great services to the party, to the working class and to the international workers' movement'.

By contrast, in preliminary discussion, Khrushchev had said: 'Stalin destroyed the party. He was not a Marxist. He wiped out all that is sacred in a human being.' Later, fearing that the truth about Stalin could lead to criticism of the political system, Khrushchev reverted to saying that Stalin had been a staunch revolutionary. Such contradictions are evidence of a hard-fought battle – a struggle that should not be seen as mere palace intrigue. It took resolve and courage, qualities that Khrushchev showed in presenting the report and then also in exonerating innocent prisoners and instituting controls over the security apparatus. Despite resistance, Khrushchev had Stalin's body removed from the mausoleum.

After the 20th Congress, policies underwent considerable change. A new doctrine proclaimed the possibility of preventing a third world war, of ending the Cold War and of peaceful revolution. Democratisation of society, known as the thaw, enabled Aleksandr Solzhenitsyn to publish *One Day in the Life of Ivan Denisovich*. I remember the appearance of truthful and moving films such as *The Cranes Are Flying*, and hundreds of grateful listeners flocking to the Polytechnic Museum to listen to readings of the young poets Yevgeny Yevtushenko, Andrey Voznesensky and Robert Rozhdestvensky.

Of course the old political system constrained what Khrushchev could do. Besides, he remained a man of his times – hence his conflict with the intelligentsia, and his aggressive speech at the United Nations. Yet, Khrushchev was a man of the people: his housing policies enabled millions who used to languish in communal flats, huts and basements to get free apartments; he put an end to Stalin's virtual 'serfdom' in the countryside; and he tried to reform the economy and the party's vertical structure. He did not succeed in the latter – the party *nomenklatura* rejected his efforts. Later, the party's upper echelons did their best to remove him from power.

Nevertheless, Khrushchev's achievements were remarkable. His 20th Congress speech and his reforms were the first blow struck at what had seemed an unshakable totalitarian system. Perestroika continued what the 20th Congress had started, seeking to give back to socialism the 'human face' destroyed by Stalin. By laying the foundations of a social market economy and by instituting free speech and elections, Perestroika implemented a new social-democratic project. Its completion was thwarted by the conservatives' putsch followed by the actions of right-wing radicals led by Boris Yeltsin, who dismantled the Soviet Union and subjected the people to a 'shock experiment'. The result was the emergence of a 'wild capitalism' which brought with it impoverishment, crime and corrupt government.

Some became nostalgic for the past. There are frequent media calls for a return to a Stalinist 'iron hand'. Films and books have depicted Stalin not as a tyrant, but as a wise father of the people. Much has changed for the better under Vladimir Putin. Once again, people have hopes, and they support the president. Russia is looking for its own path to the future. I believe that the first steps on this path were taken at the 20th Congress, when Nikita Khrushchev revealed the stunning truth about how Stalin and his blood-stained regime set back our country's development.

The cult of the individual

NIKITA KHRUSHCHEV
February 25 1956

Comrades! In the party central committee's report at the 20th Congress and in a number of speeches by delegates to the Congress a lot has been said about the cult of the individual. After Stalin's death, the central committee began explaining that it is foreign to the spirit of Marxism-Leninism to elevate one person, to transform him into a superman possessing supernatural characteristics, akin to those of a god. Such a man supposedly knows everything, sees everything, thinks for everyone, can do anything, is infallible in his behaviour. Such a belief about a man, and specifically about Stalin, was cultivated among us for many years. The objective of this report is not a thorough evaluation of Stalin's life and activity. Concerning Stalin's merits, an entirely sufficient number of books, pamphlets and studies had already been written in his lifetime. Stalin's role in the execution of the socialist revolution, in the civil war, and in the construction of socialism is universally known.

At present, we are concerned with how the cult of Stalin has been gradually growing, the cult which became the source of a whole series of exceedingly serious perversions of party principles, of party democracy, of revolutionary legality. The central committee considers it absolutely necessary to make material pertaining to this matter available to the 20th Congress.

The great modesty of the genius of the revolution, Vladimir Ilyich Lenin, is known. Lenin always stressed the role of the people as the creator of history. Lenin mercilessly stigmatised every manifestation of the cult of the individual. Lenin never imposed his views by force. He tried to convince. He patiently explained his opinions to others.

Lenin detected in Stalin those negative characteristics which resulted later in grave consequences. Fearing the future fate of the Soviet nation, Lenin pointed out that it was necessary to consider transferring Stalin from the position of general secretary because Stalin did not have a proper attitude toward his comrades. In 1922 Vladimir Ilyich wrote: 'After taking over the position of general secretary, comrade Stalin accumulated immeasurable power in his hands and I am not certain whether he will be always able to use this power with the required care.' Vladimir Ilyich said: 'I propose that the comrades consider the method by which Stalin would be removed from this position and by which another man would be selected for it, a man who, above all, would differ from Stalin in only one quality, namely, greater toler- ance, greater loyalty, greater kindness.'

Comrades! The party Congress should become acquainted

with new documents, which confirm Stalin's character. In March 1923, Lenin sent Stalin the following letter: 'Dear comrade Stalin! You permitted yourself a rude summons of my wife to the telephone and a rude reprimand of her. Despite the fact that she told you that she agreed to forget what was said, I have no intention to forget so easily.' Comrades! I will not comment on these documents. They speak eloquently for themselves.

As later events have proven, Lenin's anxiety was justified. Stalin, who absolutely did not tolerate collegiality in leadership and in work, acted not through persuasion, but by imposing his concepts and demanding absolute submission to his opinion. Stalin originated the concept 'enemy of the people'. This term automatically made it unnecessary that the ideological errors of a man be proven. It made possible the use of the cruellest repression, against anyone who in any way disagreed with Stalin, against those who were only suspected of hostile intent, against those who had bad reputations. On the whole, the only proof of guilt actually used was the 'confession' of the accused himself. 'Confessions' were acquired through physical pressures. Innocent individuals – who in the past had defended the party line – became victims. Mass arrests and deportations of many thousands of people, execution without trial and without normal investigation created conditions of insecurity, fear and even desperation.

Vladimir Ilyich demanded uncompromising dealings with the enemies of the revolution. Lenin used such methods, however, only against actual class enemies and not against those who blunder. Stalin, on the other hand, used extreme methods and mass repressions at a time when the revolution was already victorious. During Lenin's life, party congresses were convened regularly. Lenin considered it absolutely necessary that the party discuss at length all questions bearing on the development of government. After Lenin's death, Stalin trampled on the principle of collective party leadership. Of the 139 members and candidates of the central committee who were elected at the 17th Congress, 98 persons, 70%, were arrested and shot. It is inconceivable that a Congress so composed could have elected a central committee in which a majority would prove to be enemies of the party. Delegates were active participants in the building of our socialist state; many of them suffered and fought during the pre-revolutionary years; they fought their enemies valiantly and often nervelessly looked into the face of death.

How, then, can we believe that such people had joined the camps of the enemies of socialism? This was the result of the abuse of power by Stalin. On the evening of December 1 1934 on Stalin's initiative, the secretary of the presidium signed the following directive: '1. Investigative agencies are directed to speed up the cases of those accused of acts of terror; 2. Judicial organs are directed not to hold up execution in order to consider pardon; 3. The organs of the commissariat of internal affairs are directed to execute the death sentences immediately after the passage of sentences.' This directive became the basis for mass acts of abuse. The accused were deprived of any possibility that their cases might be re-examined, even when they stated before the court that their 'confessions' were secured by force.

Lenin taught that the application of revolutionary violence is necessitated by the resistance of the exploiting classes, and this referred to the era when the exploiting classes existed and were powerful. As soon as the nation's political situation had improved, when in January 1920 the Red Army took Rostov, Lenin gave instructions to stop mass terror and to abolish the death penalty. Stalin deviated from these precepts. Terror was actually directed not at the remnants of the defeated exploiting classes but against the honest workers of the party; against them were made lying, slanderous and absurd accusations. Mass repressions contributed to the spreading of unhealthy suspicion, and sowed distrust among communists.

Stalin was a very distrustful man, sickly suspicious. He could look at a man and say: 'Why are your eyes so shifty today?' or 'Why are you turning so much today and avoiding to look me directly in the eyes?' The sickly suspicion created in him a general distrust. Everywhere and in everything he saw 'enemies', 'two-facers' and 'spies'. Stalin dispatched a coded telegram on January 20 1939 to the committee secretaries of provinces and regions. This telegram stated: 'It is known that all bourgeois intelligence services use methods of physical influence against representatives of the socialist proletariat. The question arises as to why the socialist intelligence service should be more humanitarian against the mad agents of the bourgeoisie. The central committee considers that physical pressure should be used obligatorily against known enemies of the people.' Thus, Stalin sanctioned the most brutal violation of socialist legality, torture and oppression.

The power accumulated in the hands of one person, Stalin, led to serious consequences during the great patriotic war. When we look at many of our novels, films and historical-scientific studies, the role of Stalin in the patriotic war appears to be entirely improbable. Stalin had foreseen everything. The epic victory is ascribed as being completely due to the strategic genius of Stalin. What are the facts of this matter? Stalin advanced the thesis that our nation experienced an 'unexpected' attack by the Germans. But, comrades, this is completely untrue. As soon as Hitler came to power he assigned to himself the task of liquidating communism. The fascists were saying this openly. They did not hide their plans.

Despite grave warnings, the necessary steps were not taken to prepare. We paid with great losses – until our generals succeeded in altering the situation. Stalin tried to inculcate the notion that the victories gained by the Soviet nation were all due to the courage, daring, and genius of Stalin and of no one else. Let us take our military films. They make us feel sick. Let us recall *The Fall of Berlin*. Here only Stalin acts. He issues orders in a hall in which there are many empty chairs. And where is the military command? Where is the politburo? Where is the government? What are they doing, and with what are they engaged? There is nothing about them in the film. Stalin acts for everybody, he does not reckon with anyone. He asks no one for advice. Everything is shown to the people in this false light. Why? To surround Stalin with glory – contrary to historical truth. Not Stalin, but the party as a whole, the Soviet government, our heroic army, its talented leaders and brave soldiers, the whole Soviet nation – these are the ones who assured victory in the great patriotic war. The magnificent, heroic deeds of hundreds of millions of people of the east and of the west during the fight against the threat of fascist subjugation which loomed before us will live for centuries, for millennia in the memory of thankful humanity.

Comrades! The cult of the individual acquired such monstrous size chiefly because Stalin himself supported the glorification of his own person. The edition of his short biography, which was published in 1948, is an expression of the most dissolute flattery, approved and edited by Stalin personally. He marked the very places where he thought that the praise of his services was insufficient. Here are some examples characterising Stalin's activity, added in Stalin's own hand, 'The guiding force of the party and the state was comrade Stalin'. Thus writes Stalin himself! Then he adds: 'Although he performed his tasks as leader of the people with consummate skill, Stalin never allowed his work to be marred by the slightest hint of vanity, conceit or self-adulation.' Where and when could a leader so praise himself?

Comrades! The cult of the individual brought about rude violation of party democracy, sterile administration, deviations of all sorts, cover-ups of shortcomings, and varnishings of reality. Our nation bore forth many flatterers and special-ists in false optimism and deceit.

Some comrades may ask us: Where were the members of the politburo? Why did they not assert themselves against the cult of the individual in time? And why is this being done only now? First of all, members of the politburo viewed these matters in a different way at different times. Initially, many backed Stalin actively because he was one of the strongest Marxists and his logic, his strength and his will greatly influenced party work. After Lenin's death, especially during the first years, Stalin actively fought for Leninism against the enemies of Leninist theory and against those who deviated. At that time the party had to fight those who tried to lead the country away from the correct Leninist path. It had to fight Trotskyites, Zinovievites and rightists, and bourgeois nationalists. This fight was indispensable. Later, however, Stalin began to fight honest Soviet people. Attempts to oppose groundless suspicions and charges resulted in the opponent's falling victim to the repression.

Comrades! So as not to repeat errors of the past, the central committee has declared itself resolutely against the cult of the individual. We consider that Stalin was extolled to excess. However, in the past Stalin undoubtedly performed great services to the party, to the working class and to the inter-national workers' movement. Comrades! Lenin had often stressed that modesty is an absolutely integral part of a real Bolshevik. Lenin himself was the living personification of the greatest modesty. We cannot say that we have been following this Leninist example in all respects. We must correct this. But this should be done calmly. We cannot let this matter get out of the party, especially not to the press. It is for this reason that we are considering it here at a closed Congress session. We should not give ammunition to the enemy; we should not wash our dirty linen before their eyes.

Comrades! We must abolish the cult of the individual once and for all. We must correct the views connected with the cult in history, philosophy and sciences, and continue systematically the work done by the party's central committee during the last years, a work characterised by collective leadership and self-criticism.

Comrades! The 20th Congress of the Communist party of the Soviet Union has manifested with a new strength the unshakable unity of our party, its cohesiveness around the central committee, its resolute will to accomplish the great task of building communism. And the fact that we present in all their ramifications the basic problems of overcoming the cult of the individual is evidence of the great moral and political strength of our party. We are absolutely certain that our party, armed with the historical resolutions of the 20th Congress, will lead the Soviet people along the Leninist path to new successes, to new victories. Long live the victorious banner of our party – Leninism!

Reprinted with the permission of the family of Nikita Khrushchev.

This report appeared in the *Manchester Guardian* on
March 17 1956 – three weeks after the speech – when a
copy was smuggled to the west.

SHEDDING NEW LIGHT ON
THE STALIN REGIME

Khrushchev's reported revelations to the party congress

A bitter attack on Stalin accusing him of responsibility for
massacre and torture during his 30 years in power has been
made by Mr Khrushchev, according to reports from reliable
Communist sources reaching here [Bonn]. These reports said
that he charged Stalin with crimes never before mentioned in
the Soviet Union.

The attack on Stalin came in a long speech by the
Communist party leader to the security session of the recent
party Congress on February 25, the day before the Congress
ended. During the session Khrushchev is said to have painted
a vivid picture to the delegates of the regime of 'suspicion, fear
and terror' through which Stalin ruled. He also held Stalin
responsible for Soviet failure in the early stages of the war
both by ignoring warnings and by 'weakening' the country's
morale and economy in the great pre-war purges.

Breaking the 'cult'

The decision to throw open the terrible detailed secrets of the Stalin era was reached because it was felt to be the only way of breaking the magic of the 'Stalin cult'. An edited and slightly shortened version of the speech is said to have been produced for the public. At the same time, a highly secret document was prepared from Stalin's archives for members of the Central Committee only. In his speech Khrushchev was reported to have declared that Stalin decimated the Communist party by purges. Five thousand of the Red Army's best officers were 'murdered'.

According to the report, Khrushchev also referred to the fate of some Soviet leaders. There was suspicion, he said, that Stalin was implicated in the assassination in 1934 of Kirov, the Leningrad party chief. About three-quarters of the delegates to the 17th party Congress, many of whom spoke against Stalin, were shot. After Lenin's death Stalin insulted and threatened his widow. He told her, if she continued to speak against him in public he would issue a declaration that she had never been Lenin's wife and put someone else in her place.

Warnings ignored

Khrushchev was also quoted as saying that before the German attack in 1941 everyone knew that war was coming except Stalin, who refused to believe it. He ignored the warnings of Mr Churchill and the Soviet military attaché in Berlin, who knew and informed Moscow of the exact date of the coming attack. When the attack came, his first order to his troops was not to return the fire. Such was his faith in Hitler that he informed the Red Army that the attack was nothing but 'indiscipline' on the part of certain German units.

The reports quoted Khrushchev as saying that after the war Stalin became especially suspicious, and in the later period of his life an atmosphere of 'fear and terror' prevailed. Even politburo members lived in fear. Stalin humiliated Khrushchev himself at a reception at which foreigners were present.

Mania and conceit

Stalin, he went on, was ruled by a mixture of persecution mania and gross conceit. One of his favourite occupations was watching a film called *Unforgettable 1919* in which he was shown riding in an armoured car brandishing a sword as bullets whistled by. He is reported to have described Stalin's 'biography' as an 'odious book'. He was said to have told how Stalin, in editing the book, inserted phrases describing him as a 'shy and modest person'.

During Khrushchev's description of some of the worse aspects of Stalin's rule of terror, some delegates were reported to have shouted: 'How did you stand it? Why didn't you kill him?' Khrushchev is reported to have replied: 'What could we do? There was a reign of terror. You just had to look at him wrongly and the next day you lost your head.' The report added that some 30 of the 1,600 delegates fainted during or after Khrushchev's speech.

Weapons for squalid and trivial ends

ANEURIN BEVAN
December 5 1956

This is an edited version of a speech
Aneurin Bevan delivered to the House of
Commons on December 5 1956.

For ease of reading, individual excisions are not marked,
nor is it indicated when the case of a letter changes
due to the deletion of part of a sentence.

Full text in Hansard, December 5 1956, columns 1268–1283.

Tam Dalyell

Tam Dalyell was the Labour MP for Linlithgow
until 2005 and is a vocal critic of the 2003
invasion of Iraq.

As a speaker at an evening meeting at Leeds University, I was
invited to stay the night with the vice-chancellor Lord Boyle,
who as Sir Edward Boyle had been minister of education in
the Conservative government. Over a nightcap, I asked him
whose was the greatest speech he had ever heard in the House
of Commons. Unhesitatingly, he said 'Nye Bevan on Suez'.
Boyle was not alone in this opinion. In Mr Speaker's House,
I heard Selwyn Lloyd reminisce that Bevan's Suez speech was
the greatest Commons performance, 'and it was at my expense,
because as foreign secretary, it had been my duty to speak
before him and put the government's case.' So, it was not only
loyal Bevanites who judged Nye's 49-minute tour de force as
the greatest of speeches; it was also opponents and victims.

Why? An amalgam of reasons. First, to hear Nye Bevan, as I did at rallies, such as his visit to the Guildhall in Cambridge in early 1956, was magic – the lilting Welsh voice, the imaginative language and imagery, the timing, the use of his stammer to huge effect, and the impeccable good manners, even when delivering withering scorn.

Second, there was the robustness. As a no-hoper Labour candidate in the 1959 election, I went to a party briefing, where we were given sessions with Hugh Gaitskell, Harold Wilson and other luminaries of the day. It was Nye who charmed us. Always, he urged, take the strongest part of your opponent's case, not the weakest. This is exactly what he did and is why so many of his speeches can be classed as great. And on this occasion he had a most powerful case to make. After Egypt nationalised the Suez canal, the Eden government had, in Bevan's phrase, 'cooked up' circumstances to allow it to 'send in the troops'. The move was fraught with danger, and soon proved politically calamitous once the US forced the invaders to a ceasefire. But Suez also reflected outmoded imperialist assumptions, which, with great precision, Bevan exposed and demolished.

Bevan's Suez speech resonates today. He told the Commons that he had been looking through the various reasons that the government had given for making war on Egypt. It really was desirable, Bevan told the House, that when a nation makes war upon another, it should be quite clear why it was doing so. The government should not keep changing the reasons as time goes on. Half a century ago he was saying that there was no correspondence between the reasons given at the fag end of the Suez crisis, and the reasons set out by the prime minister at the beginning. The reasons changed all the time.

Does that not echo today in the wake of the whole Iraqi debacle? This is not the occasion to reiterate all the various so-called reasons that have been deployed since the one that first swayed the House of Commons, namely that there were weapons of mass destruction, likely to be used by Saddam Hussein. (I never believed a word of what the prime minister was saying; as early as September 2002 a cartoon appeared of me holding up the dossier and demanding it be put up for the Booker Prize for fiction.) The situation was little different at the time of Suez for a group of Bevanite MPs from the left of the party – and indeed for some Conservatives drowned out by their colleagues, but who knew the Arab world.

Bevan homed in on the issue of intelligence. Britain had sent an ultimatum to Egypt by which we had told it that unless it agreed to our landing in Ismailia, Suez and Port Said, we should make war upon it. We knew very well, did we not, that Egypt's leader, Gamal Abdel Nasser, could not possibly comply? Did we really believe he was going to give in at once? Was our information from Egypt so bad that we did not know that an ultimatum was bound to consolidate his position at home and in the whole Arab world?

In 1964, while on my honeymoon in Egypt, I was woken by a nervous Egyptian at midnight saying that an important man wished to see me. I was whisked out to see President Nasser, who, quite often working in the cool of the night, would see foreigners at unearthly hours. He came into the room with the words: 'We know about you, that your mother and father spoke Arabic. Why don't you?' I could only give a watery smile and said I would try. He said one of the troubles was that many leading people in Britain knew little of the aspirations of the Arab world. He said he was sad that Aneurin Bevan had died, and referred to a phrase Bevan used about the whole Arab world being driven into one solid phalanx by the rump of the United Nations, by which he meant the Western powers.

Plus ça change ...

Weapons for squalid
and trivial ends

ANEURIN BEVAN
December 5 1956

The speech to which we have just listened is the last of a
long succession that the right honourable gentleman, the
Secretary of State for foreign affairs, has made to the House
in the last few months and, if I may be allowed to say so,
I congratulate him upon having survived so far. He appears
to be in possession of vigorous health, which is obviously
not enjoyed by all his colleagues, and he appears also to be
exempted from those Freudian lapses which have distin-
guished the speeches of the Lord Privy Seal, and therefore
he has survived so far with complete vigour. However, I am
bound to say that the speech by the right honourable
gentleman today carries the least conviction of all.

I have been looking through the various objectives and
reasons that the government have given to the House of
Commons for making war on Egypt, and it really is desirable that when a nation makes war upon another nation it
should be quite clear why it does so. It should not keep

changing the reasons as time goes on. There is, in fact, no correspondence whatsoever between the reasons given today and the reasons set out by the prime minister at the beginning. The reasons have changed all the time. I have got a list of them here, and for the sake of the record I propose to read it. I admit that I found some difficulty in organising a speech with any coherence because of the incoherence of the reasons. They are very varied.

On October 30, the prime minister said that the purpose was, first, 'to seek to separate the combatants'; second, 'to remove the risk to free passage through the canal'. The speech we have heard today is the first speech in which that subject has been dropped. We have heard from the right honourable and learned gentleman today a statement which I am quite certain all the world will read with astonishment. He has said that when we landed in Port Said there was already every reason to believe that both Egypt and Israel had agreed to cease fire. The minister shakes his head, if he will recollect what his right honourable and learned friend said, it was that there was still a doubt about the Israeli reply. Are we really now telling this country and the world that all these calamitous consequences have been brought down upon us merely because of a doubt? That is what he said.

In the history of nations, there is no example of such frivolity. When I have looked at this chronicle of events during the last few days, with every desire in the world to understand it, I just have not been able to understand the mentality of the government. We are telling the nation and the world that, having decided upon the course, we went on with it despite the fact that the objective we had set ourselves had already been achieved, namely, the separation of the combatants.

As to the objective of removing the risk to free passage through the canal, I must confess that I have been astonished at this also. We sent an ultimatum to Egypt by which we told her that unless she agreed to our landing in Ismailia, Suez and Port Said, we should make war upon her. We knew very well, did we not, that Nasser could not possibly comply? Did we really believe that Nasser was going to give in at once? Is our information from Egypt so bad that we did not know that an ultimatum of that sort was bound to consolidate his position in Egypt and in the whole Arab world? Did we really believe that Nasser was going to wait for us to arrive? He did what anybody would have thought he would do, and if the government did not think he would do it, on that account alone they ought to resign. He sank ships in the canal, the wicked man. The result is that the first objective realised was the opposite of the one we set out to achieve; the canal was blocked, and it is still blocked.

On October 31, the prime minister said that our object was to secure a lasting settlement and to protect our nationals. What do we think of that? In the meantime, our nationals were living in Egypt while we were murdering Egyptians at Port Said. We left our nationals in Egypt at the mercy of what might have been riots throughout the country. We were still voyaging through the Mediterranean, after having exposed them to risk by our own behaviour. What does the House believe that the country will think when it really comes to understand all this? On November 1, we were told the reason was 'to stop hostilities' and 'prevent a resumption of them'. But hostilities had already been practically stopped. On November 3, our objectives became much more ambitious – 'to deal with all the outstanding problems in the Middle East'.

In the famous book *Madame Bovary* there is a story of a woman who goes from one sin to another, a long story of moral decline. In this case, our ambitions soar the farther away we are from realising them. Our objective was, 'to deal with all the outstanding problems in the Middle East'. After having insulted the United States, after having affronted all our friends in the Commonwealth, after having driven the whole of the Arab world into one solid phalanx behind Nasser, we were then going to deal with all the outstanding problems in the Middle East.

The next objective of which we were told was to ensure that the Israeli forces withdrew from Egyptian territory. That, I understand, is what we were there for. We went into Egyptian territory in order to establish our moral right to make the Israelis clear out. That is a remarkable war aim, is it not? To establish our case before the eyes of the world, Israel being the wicked invader, we being the nice friend of Egypt, went to protect her from the Israelis, but, unfortunately, we had to bomb the Egyptians first.

On November 6, the prime minister said: 'The action we

took has been an essential condition for a United Nations force to come into the Canal Zone itself.' That is one of the most remarkable claims of all. It is, of course, exactly the same claim which might have been made, if they had thought about it in time, by Mussolini and Hitler, that they made war on the world in order to call the United Nations into being. If it were possible for bacteria to argue with each other, they would be able to say that of course their chief justification was the advancement of medical science.

Why did we start this operation? We started this operation in order to give Nasser a black eye – if we could, to overthrow him – but, in any case, to secure control of the canal. The right honourable and learned gentleman is sufficiently aware of the seriousness of it to start his speech today with collusion. If collusion can be established, the whole fabric of the government's case falls to the ground. It is believed in the United States and it is believed by large numbers of people in Great Britain that we were well aware that Israel was going to make the attack on Egypt. In fact, very few of the activities at the beginning of October are credible except upon the assumption that the French and British governments knew that something was going to happen in Egypt. Indeed, the right honourable and learned gentleman has not been frank with the House. We have asked him over and over again. He has said, 'Ah, we did not conspire with France and Israel.' We never said that the government might have conspired. What we said was that they might have known about it.

The right honourable and learned gentleman gave the House the impression that at no time had he ever warned Israel against attack on Egypt. If we apprehend trouble of these dimensions – we are not dealing with small matters – if we apprehend that the opening phases of a third world war might start or turn upon an attack by Israel on anyone, why did we not make it quite clear to Israel?

The fact is, that all these long telephone conversations and conferences between M Guy Mollet, M Pineau [respectively, France's prime minister and foreign minister] and the prime minister are intelligible only on the assumption that something was being cooked up. All the time there was this coming and going between ourselves and the French government. Did the French know? It is believed in France that the French knew about the Israeli intention. If the French knew, did they tell the British government? Every circumstantial fact that we know points to that conclusion. What happened? Did Marianne take John Bull to an unknown rendezvous? Did Marianne say to John Bull that there was a forest fire going to start, and did John Bull then say, 'We ought to put it out,' but Marianne said, 'No, let us warm our hands by it. It is a nice fire'? Did Marianne deceive John Bull or seduce him?

Now I would conclude by saying this. I do not believe that any of us yet have realised the complete change that has taken place in the relationship between nations and between governments and peoples. These were objectives, I do beg honourable members to reflect, that were not realisable by the means that we adopted. These civil, social and political objectives in modern society are not attainable by armed force. Even if we had occupied Egypt by armed force we could not have secured the freedom of passage through the canal. It is clear that there is such xenophobia, that there is such passion, that there is such bitter feeling against Western imperialism – rightly or wrongly: I am not arguing the merits at the moment – among millions of people that they are not prepared to keep the arteries of European commerce alive and intact if they themselves want to cut them. We could not keep ships going through the canal. The canal is too easily sabotaged, if Egypt wants to sabotage it. Why on earth did we imagine that the objectives could be realised in that way in the middle of the 20th century?

The social furniture of modern society is so complicated and fragile that it cannot support the jackboot. We cannot run the processes of modern society by attempting to impose our will upon nations by armed force. If we have not learned that, we have learned nothing. Therefore, from our point of view here, whatever may have been the morality of the government's action, there is no doubt about its imbecility. There is not the slightest shadow of doubt that we have attempted to use methods which were bound to destroy the objectives we had, and, of course, this is what we have discovered.

I commend to honourable members, if they have not seen it, a very fine cartoon in *Punch* by Illingworth and called

Desert Victory. There we see a black, ominous, sinister background and a pipeline broken, pouring oil into the desert sands. How on earth do honourable members opposite imagine that hundreds of miles of pipeline can be kept open if the Arabs do not want it to be kept open? It is not enough to say that there are large numbers of Arabs who want the pipeline to be kept open because they live by it. It has been proved over and over again now in the modern world that men and women are often prepared to put up with material losses for things that they really think worthwhile. It has been shown in Budapest, and it could be shown in the Middle East. That is why I beg honourable members to turn their backs on this most ugly chapter and realise that if we are to live in the world and are to be regarded as a decent nation, decent citizens in the world, we have to act up to different standards than the one that we have been following in the last few weeks.

I resent most bitterly this unconcern for the lives of innocent men and women. It may be that the dead in Port Said are 100, 200 or 300. If it is only one, we had no business to take it. Do honourable members begin to realise how this is going to revolt the world when it passes into the imagination of men and women everywhere that we – with eight million here in London, the biggest single civilian target in the world, with our crowded island exposed, as no nation in the world is exposed, to the barbarism of modern weapons – we ourselves set the example. We ourselves conscript our boys and put guns and aeroplanes in their hands and say,

'Bomb there.' Really, this is so appalling that human language can hardly describe it. And for what?

The government resorted to epic weapons for squalid and trivial ends, and that is why, all through this unhappy period, ministers, all of them, have spoken and argued and debated well below their proper form – because they have been synthetic villains. They are not really villains. They have only set off on a villainous course, and they cannot even use the language of villainy.

Therefore, in conclusion, I say that it is no use honourable members consoling themselves that they have more support in the country than many of them feared they might have. Of course they have support in the country. They have support among many of the unthinking and unreflective who still react to traditional values, who still think that we can solve all these problems in the old ways. Of course they have. Not all the human race has grown to adult state yet. But do not let them take comfort in that thought. The right honourable member for Woodford (Sir Winston Churchill) has warned them before. In the first volume of his *Second World War*, he writes about the situation before the war and he says this: 'Thus an administration more disastrous than any in our history saw all its errors and shortcomings acclaimed by the nation. There was, however, a bill to be paid, and it took the new House of Commons nearly 10 years to pay it.'

It will take us very many years to live down what we have done. It will take us many years to pay the price. I know that tomorrow evening honourable and right honourable members will probably, as they have done before, give the government a vote of confidence, but they know in their heart of hearts that it is a vote which the government do not deserve.

This report ran in the *Manchester Guardian*
on December 6 1956.

MR BEVAN INDICTS THE
'SYNTHETIC VILLAINS'
Wit reinforces reasoned attack on Egyptian action

Mr Selwyn Lloyd was bound to seem pedestrian beside
Mr Bevan. He was unfortunate to be drawn against Labour's
brilliant swordsman in the opening round of the two-day
contest on Suez. Here was Mr Bevan with his quicksilver
dialectical gifts presented with such a case against a government as will probably not fall to him again in his lifetime.

He jumped to his chance and for an hour employed every
weapon in his armoury – raillery, sarcasm, and wit. These
were his auxiliaries in developing what was, fundamentally,
a closely reasoned indictment of the government. He held
the House captive. The light Celtic voice, the trick of
brushing back a fallen forelock from his brow, the mannerism
of driving an argument home by stabbing the air with an
index finger – the House experienced all this, and so felt
the full impact of the man's personality.

There was no savage invective. How little provocative he
was was to be seen in the little interruption he suffered. He
sat down to a great surge of Labour cheers, Mr Gaitskell

shook him by the hand. Mr James Griffiths was too moved to have a clear idea of how to show his admiration.

The Old Claim

Mr Selwyn Lloyd strove to substantiate his claims that the government had stopped a war and compelled the UN to set up an international force. This was preceded by a documented attempt to prove that there had been no collusion with Israel. It really resolved itself into the old claim that the government did not incite Israel. This, in the eyes of Mr Bevan, fell short of a denial that the government had knowledge that Israel was to attack Egypt. [The foreign secretary's] contention that there would have been no UN force but for our intervention met with nothing but mocking laughter. His speech could not save him from cries of 'Resign' when he concluded.

'Freudian lapses'

Mr Bevan began merrily enough by shedding a new light on the mystery of Mr Butler. If Mr Bevan is right, much in Mr Butler's behaviour is to be explained by 'Freudian lapses'. That amused everybody, including Mr Butler. The member for Ebbw Vale moved into action with an inimitably satirical examination of the changing objectives which the government assigned to its operations, coupled with an exposure of how in failing to attain them the government had managed to insult the United States, affront Commonwealth countries, and make the Arab nations pro-Nasser.

Certainly, none of this was new, but in Mr Bevan's hands it became both diverting and damaging to the Government. Mr Bevan also applied himself to the charge of collusion. He could not find the coming and going between French and British ministers explicable except on the hypothesis that something was being cooked up. Did the French know, he asked. Did they tell the British Government that there was to be an attack on Egypt?

Then Mr Bevan, to everybody's entertainment, transposed his inquiries to a key of pure comedy. Did Marianne take John Bull to an unknown rendezvous? All this was done in a light, lilting voice amid shouts of laughter. And then the crown: Did Marianne deceive John Bull or seduce him? The laughter now was unbounded.

Mr Bevan was not without his serious moments. He returned to his old theme that in this changing world, people are seeking social and political ends that cannot be realised by armed force.

Not long afterwards Captain Waterhouse, the leader of the Suez Tories, was announcing that he would abstain on tonight's division [and] Mr Angus Maude said he could not give an unconditional vote of confidence to the Government.

The wind of change

HAROLD MACMILLAN
February 3 1960

This is an edited version of Harold Macmillan's
speech to the Houses of Parliament, Cape Town,
South Africa, on February 3 1960.

For ease of reading, individual excisions are not marked,
nor is it indicated when the case of a letter changes
due to the deletion of part of a sentence.

The complete speech can be found in
Pointing the Way 1959–1961,
Harold Macmillan (Macmillan, 1972).

Douglas Hurd

Douglas Hurd was Foreign Secretary 1989–1995.
His biography of Robert Peel was
published in June 2007.

No serving British prime minister had visited Africa before
Harold Macmillan set out there. He travelled in a slow
turboprop Britannia aircraft and was away for six weeks. He
joked his only purpose was escaping the British winter. In
fact the politics of Britain required him to take a close personal
interest in Africa. The course of British policy was already
set. Macmillan visited Ghana, which had been independent
for three years, and Nigeria, which was soon to follow. Others
would do the same. British ministers were transforming the
British Empire into a voluntary Commonwealth.

The main difficulty arose due to the substantial number
of white settlers. The position in Southern Rhodesia, already
self-governing with a largely white electorate, was dangerous.

And then there loomed South Africa, a full Commonwealth member but committed to rigid apartheid. The shadow of apartheid hung over the continent, frustrating at every turn efforts to persuade African nationalists that the West, rather than the Soviet Union, should be their model.

When he addressed the South African parliament, Macmillan could have offered benign reflections, praised the country's remarkable beauty or stressed the importance of trading links. In his speech he did all these things, but he also decided to give some important messages. The speech was properly constructed in an old-fashioned way. Those who advised on the text were, like Harold Macmillan himself, highly intelligent people steeped in a classical education who believed instinctively in the power of words, provided, of course, they were carefully weighed and assembled by experts. As was his habit, the prime minister illustrated the importance of the speech by being violently sick just before delivering it.

He spoke for 50 minutes, long even by the standards of the age. Most of the speech was wrapping paper; inside were two messages. The first was the celebrated claim that 'the wind of change is blowing through this continent'. By the wind of change, Macmillan meant, of course, the strength of African national consciousness. Nationalism was a fact that policies must respect. There would be no going back. Any other course would strengthen the danger of Africa going communist.

Macmillan then switched to his second message about

South Africa itself. Referring to African nationalism, he said: 'Of course, you understand this better than anyone.' By this was meant: 'You need to understand this more than anyone, but I doubt you do.' With careful words, Macmillan explained that Britain could not support apartheid. He ruled out a trade boycott, but he used quotations from St Paul and John Donne to contradict the central argument of South African foreign policy, that they had the right to do whatever they liked in their own country. He ended with an appeal to friendship. In a typical phrase he referred to himself and his colleagues as 'fleeting transient phantoms on the great stage of history' with no right to sweep aside that friendship that was the legacy of history. One more familiar quotation, this time from Burke, and he was done.

Macmillan's immediate white South African audience, for a day or two, was seduced by the prime minister's courtesy. Elsewhere, the impact became immediately clear. Britain would never stand with South Africa against African nationalism. As more colonies became independent, the contrast with apartheid would grow starker. Britain was keen to retain friendship with South Africa but would not be able or willing to shelter it from the wind of change.

British policy towards South Africa was controversial in the 34 years of apartheid that remained. We argued fiercely about joining in with sanctions. This argument obscured the continuity of British policy. Macmillan's successors followed the line set out in the Cape Town speech. Margaret Thatcher, while opposed to sanctions, made clear that Britain neither supported apartheid nor believed it could succeed. Because this continuity was understood, Britain could take a helpful part in bringing South African parties together during the last years of apartheid. We established a good relationship with President Nelson Mandela's government more quickly than most outsiders thought possible.

Macmillan spoke at Cape Town in the heyday of his power. The speech contained some of the affectations that went with his character, as well as the cadences of a generation long past. But it deserves its place as one of the defining statements of British policy in the 20th century.

The wind of change

HAROLD MACMILLAN
February 3 1960

It is a great privilege to be invited to address the members of both houses of parliament in the Union of South Africa. It is a unique privilege to do so in 1960, just half a century after the parliament of the union came to birth. I am most grateful to you all for giving me this opportunity. My tour of Africa – parts of Africa – the first ever made by a British prime minister in office, is now, alas, nearing its end, but it is fitting that it should culminate in the union parliament here in Cape Town, in this historic city so long Europe's gateway to the Indian Ocean, and to the east.

As in all the other countries that I have visited, my stay has been all too short. I wish it had been possible for me to spend a longer time here, to see more of your beautiful country and to get to know more of your people, but in the past week I have travelled many hundreds of miles and met many people in all walks of life. I have been able to get at least some idea of the great beauty of your countryside, with its farms and its forests, mountains and rivers, and the clear skies and wide horizons of the veld. Some of the younger members of my staff have told me that it has been a heavy programme, but I can assure you that my wife and I have enjoyed every moment of it. Moreover, we have been deeply moved by the warmth of our welcome which we know is an expression of your goodwill, not just to ourselves but to all the people of Britain.

It is, as I have said, a special privilege for me to be here in 1960 when you are celebrating what I might call the golden wedding of the union. At such a time it is natural and right that you should pause to take stock of your position, to look back at what you have achieved, to look forward to what lies ahead.

In the 50 years of their nationhood, the people of South Africa have built a strong economy founded upon a healthy agriculture and thriving and resilient industries. During my visit I have been able to see something of your mining industry, on which the prosperity of the country is so firmly based. I have seen the great city of Durban, with its wonderful port, and the skyscrapers of Johannesburg, standing where 70 years ago there was nothing but the open veld. I have seen, too, the fine cities of Pretoria and Bloemfontein. This afternoon I hope to see something of your wine-growing industry, which so far I have only admired as a consumer.

No one could fail to be impressed with the immense material progress which has been achieved. That all this has been accomplished in so short a time is a striking testimony to the skill, energy and initiative of your people. We in Britain are proud of the contribution we have made to this remarkable achievement. Much of it has been financed by British capital. But that is not all. We have developed trade between us to our common advantage, and our economies are now largely interdependent. You export to us raw materials, food and gold. We in return send you consumer goods or capital equipment. We take a third of all your exports and we supply a third of all your imports. Here is a true partnership, living proof of the interdependence between nations. Britain has always been your best customer and, as your new industries develop, we believe that we can be your best partners too.

In addition to building this strong economy within your own borders, you have also played your part as an independent nation in the world. As a soldier in the First World War, and as a minister in Sir Winston Churchill's government in the second, I know personally the value of the contribution which your forces made to victory in the cause of freedom. In the testing times of war or aggression, your statesmen and your soldiers have made their influence felt far beyond the African continent.

In the postwar world now, in the no less difficult task of peace, your leaders in industry, commerce and finance continue to be prominent in world affairs today. Your readiness to provide technical assistance to the less well-developed parts of Africa is of immense help to the countries that receive it. It is also a source of strength to your friends in the Commonwealth and elsewhere in the western world. You are collaborating in the work of the Commission for Technical Cooperation in Africa South of the Sahara, and now in the United Nations Economic Commission for Africa. Your minister for external affairs intends to visit Ghana later this year. All this proves your determination, as the most advanced industrial country of the continent, to play your part in the new Africa of today.

Sir, as I have travelled round the union I have found everywhere, as I expected, a deep preoccupation with what is happening in the rest of the African continent. I understand and sympathise with your interest in these events, and your anxiety about them. Ever since the break-up of the Roman Empire, one of the constant facts of political life in Europe has been the emergence of independent nations. They have come into existence over the centuries in different forms, with different kinds of government, but all have been inspired by a deep, keen feeling of nationalism, which has grown as the nations have grown.

In the 20th century, and especially since the end of the war, the processes which gave birth to the nation states of Europe have been repeated all over the world. We have seen the awakening of national consciousness in peoples who have for centuries lived in dependence upon some other power. Fifteen years ago this movement spread through Asia. Many countries there, of different races and civilisations, pressed their claim to an independent national life. Today the same thing is happening in Africa, and the most striking of all the impressions I have formed since I left London a month ago is of the strength of this African national consciousness. In different places it takes different forms, but it is happening everywhere. The wind of change is blowing through this continent, and, whether we like it or not, this growth of national consciousness is a political fact. We must all accept it as a fact, and our national policies must take account of it.

Of course, you understand this better than anyone. You are sprung from Europe, the home of nationalism, and here in Africa you have yourselves created a new nation. Indeed, in the history of our times, yours will be recorded as the first of the African nationalisms, and this tide of national consciousness which is now rising in Africa is a fact for which you and we and the other nations of the western world are ultimately responsible. For its causes are to be found in the achievements of western civilisation, in the pushing forward of the frontiers of knowledge, in the applying of science in the service of human needs, in the expanding of food production, in the speeding and multiplying of the means of communication, and perhaps, above all, the spread of education.

As I have said, the growth of national consciousness in Africa is a political fact, and we must accept it as such. That means, I would judge, that we must come to terms with it. I sincerely believe that if we cannot do so we may imperil the precarious balance between the east and west on which the peace of the world depends. The world today is divided into three main groups. First, there are what we call the western powers. You in South Africa and we in Britain belong to this group, together with our friends and allies in other parts of the Commonwealth. In the United States of America and in Europe we call it the free world. Secondly, there are the communists – Russia and her satellites in Europe and China whose population will rise by the end of the next 10 years to the staggering total of 800,000,000. Thirdly, there are those parts of the world whose people are at present uncommitted either to communism or to our western ideas.

In this context we think first of Asia and then of Africa. As I see it, the great issue in this second half of the 20th century is whether the uncommitted peoples of Asia and Africa will swing to the east or to the west. Will they be drawn into the communist camp? Or will the great experiments in self-government that are now being made in Asia and Africa, especially within the Commonwealth, prove so successful, and by their example so compelling, that the balance will come down in favour of freedom and order and justice?

The struggle is joined, and it is a struggle for the minds of men. What is now on trial is much more than our military strength or our diplomatic and administrative skill. It is our way of life. The uncommitted nations want to see before they choose. What can we show them to help them choose right? Each of the independent members of the Commonwealth must answer that question for itself. It is a basic principle of our modern Commonwealth that we respect each other's sovereignty in matters of internal policy. At the same time, we must recognise that in this shrinking world in which we live today the internal policies of one nation may have effects outside it. We may sometimes be tempted to say to each other, 'Mind your own business', but in these days I would myself expand the old saying so that it runs: 'Mind your own business, but mind how it affects my business, too.'

Let me be very frank with you, my friends. What governments and parliaments in the United Kingdom have done since the war, in according independence to India, Pakistan, Ceylon, Malaya and Ghana, and what they will do for Nigeria and other countries now nearing independence – all this, though we take full and sole responsibility for it, we do in the belief that it is the only way to establish the future of the Commonwealth and of the free world on sound foundations. All this, of course, is also of deep and close concern to you, for nothing we do in this small world can be done in a corner or remain hidden. What we do today in West, Central and East Africa becomes known tomorrow to everyone in the union, whatever his language, colour or traditions. Let me assure you, in all friendliness, that we are well aware of this and that we have acted and will act with full knowledge of the responsibility we have to all our friends.

Nevertheless, I am sure you will agree that in our own areas of responsibility we must each do what we think right. What we think right derives from a long experience both of failure and success in the management of our own affairs. We have tried to learn and apply the lessons of our judgment of right and wrong. Our justice is rooted in the same soil as yours – in Christianity and in the rule of law as the basis of a free society. This experience of our own explains why it has been our aim in the countries for which we have borne responsibility, not only to raise the material standards of living, but also to create a society which respects the rights of individuals, a society in which men are given the opportunity to grow to their full stature – and that must, in our view, include the opportunity to have an increasing share in political power and responsibility, a society in which individual merit, and individual merit alone, is the criterion for a man's advancement, whether political or economic.

Finally, in countries inhabited by several different races, it has been our aim to find means by which the community can become more of a community, and fellowship can be fostered between its various parts. This problem is by no means confined to Africa. Nor is it always a problem of a European minority. In Malaya, for instance, though there are Indian and European minorities, Malays and Chinese make up the great bulk of the population, and the Chinese are not much fewer in numbers than the Malays. Yet these two peoples must learn to live together in harmony and unity and the strength of Malaya as a nation will depend on the different contributions which the two races can make.

The attitude of the United Kingdom towards this problem was clearly expressed by the Foreign Secretary,

Mr Selwyn Lloyd, speaking at the United Nations general assembly on September 17 1959. These were his words: 'In those territories where different races or tribes live side by side, the task is to ensure that all the people may enjoy security and freedom and the chance to contribute as individuals to the progress and well-being of these countries. We reject the idea of any inherent superiority of one race over another. Our policy therefore is non-racial. It offers a future in which Africans, Europeans, Asians, the peoples of the Pacific and others with whom we are concerned, will all play their full part as citizens in the countries where they live, and in which feelings of race will be submerged in loyalty to new nations.'

I have thought you would wish me to state plainly and with full candour the policy for which we in Britain stand. It may well be that, in trying to do our duty as we see it, we shall sometimes make difficulties for you. If this proves to be so, we shall regret it. But I know that even so you would not ask us to flinch from doing our duty. You, too, will do your duty as you see it. I am well aware of the peculiar nature of the problems with which you are faced here in the Union of South Africa. I know the differences between your situation and that of most of the other states in Africa. You have here some three million people of European origin. This country is their home. It has been their home for many generations. They have no other. The same is true of Europeans in Central and East Africa. In most other African states, those who have come from Europe have come to work, to contribute their skills, perhaps to teach, but not to make a home.

The problems to which you, as members of the union parliament, have to address yourselves are very different from those which face the parliaments of countries with homogenous populations. These are complicated and baffling problems. It would be surprising if your interpretation of your duty did not sometimes produce very different results from ours in terms of government policies and actions. As a fellow member of the Commonwealth, it is our earnest desire to give South Africa our support and encouragement, but I hope you won't mind my saying frankly that there are some aspects of your policies which make it impossible for us to do this without being false to our own deep convictions about the political destinies of free men to which, in our own territories, we are trying to give effect. I think we ought, as friends, to face together, without seeking to apportion credit or blame, the fact that in the world of today this difference of outlook lies between us.

I said that I was speaking as a friend. I can also claim to be speaking as a relation, for we Scots can claim family connections with both the great European sections of your population, not only with the English-speaking people but with the Afrikaans-speaking as well. This is a point which hardly needs emphasis in Cape Town, where you can see every day the statue of that great Scotsman, Andrew Murray. His work in the Dutch Reformed Church in the Cape, and the work of his son in the Orange Free State, was among Afrikaans-speaking people.

But though I count myself a Scot, my mother was an American, and the United States provides a valuable illustration of one of the main points which I have been trying to make in my remarks today. Its population, like yours, is of different strains, and over the years most of those who have gone to North America have gone there in order to escape conditions in Europe which they found intolerable. The pilgrim fathers were fleeing from persecution as Puritans, and the Marylanders from persecution as Roman Catholics. Throughout the 19th century a stream of immigrants flowed across the Atlantic to escape from the poverty in their homelands, and in the 20th century the United States have provided asylum for the victims of political oppression in Europe.

Thus, for the majority of its inhabitants America has been a place of refuge, or a place to which people went because they wanted to get away from Europe. It is not surprising, therefore, that for many years a main objective of American statesmen, supported by the American public, was to isolate themselves from Europe, and with their great material strength, and the vast resources open to them, this might have seemed an attractive and practicable course. Nevertheless, in the two world wars of this century they have found themselves unable to stand aside. Twice their manpower in arms has streamed back across the Atlantic to shed blood in those European struggles from which their ancestors thought they would escape by emigrating to the new world; and when the second war was over they were forced to recognise that in the small world of today isolationism is out of date and offers no assurance of security.

The fact is that in this modern world no country, not even the greatest, can live for itself alone. Nearly 2,000 years ago, when the whole of the civilised world was comprised within the confines of the Roman Empire, St Paul proclaimed one of the great truths of history – we are all members one of another. During this 20th century that eternal truth has taken on a new and exciting significance. It has always been impossible for the individual man to live in isolation from his fellows, in the home, the tribe, the village, or the city. Today it is impossible for nations to live in isolation from one another. What Dr John Donne said of individual men 300 years ago is true today of my country, your country, and all the countries of the world: 'Any man's death diminishes me, because I am involved in mankind; And therefore never send to know for whom the bell tolls; it tolls for thee.'

All nations now are interdependent one upon another, and this is generally realised throughout the western world. I hope in due course the countries of communism will recognise it too. It was certainly with that thought in mind that I took the decision to visit Moscow about this time last year. Russia has been isolationist in her time and still has tendencies that way, but the fact remains that we must live in the same world with Russia, and we must find a way of doing so. I believe that the initiative which we took last year has had some success, although grave difficulties may arise.

Nevertheless, I think nothing but good can come out of its extending contacts between individuals, contacts in trade and from the exchange of visitors.

I certainly do not believe in refusing to trade with people because you may happen to dislike the way they manage their internal affairs at home. Boycotts will never get you anywhere, and may I say in parenthesis that I deprecate the attempts that are being made today in Britain to organise the consumer boycott of South African goods. It has never been the practice, as far as I know, of any government of the United Kingdom of whatever complexion to undertake or support campaigns of this kind designed to influence the internal politics of another Commonwealth country, and my colleagues in the United Kingdom deplore this proposed boycott and regard it as undesirable from every point of view. It can only have serious effects on Commonwealth relations, on trade, and lead to the ultimate detriment of others than those against whom it is aimed.

I said I was speaking of the interdependence of nations. The members of the Commonwealth feel particularly strongly the value of interdependence. They are as independent as any nation in this shrinking world can be, but they have voluntarily agreed to work together. They recognise that there may be and must be differences in their institutions, in their internal policies, and their membership does not imply the wish to express a judgment on these matters, or the need to impose a stifling uniformity. It is the flexibility of our Commonwealth institutions which gives them their strength.

Mr President, Mr Speaker, honourable ministers, ladies and gentlemen, I fear I have kept you a long time. I much welcome the opportunity to speak to this great audience. In conclusion, may I say this: I have spoken frankly about the differences between our two countries in their approach to one of the great current problems with which each has to deal within its own sphere of responsibility. These differences are well known. They are matters of public knowledge, indeed of public controversy, and I should have been less than honest if by remaining silent on them I had seemed to imply that they did not exist. But differences on one subject, important though it is, need not and should not impair our capacity to cooperate with one another in furthering the many practical interests which we share in common.

The independent members of the Commonwealth do not always agree on every subject. It is not a condition of their association that they should do so. On the contrary, the strength of our Commonwealth lies largely in the fact that it is a free association of independent sovereign states, each responsible for ordering its own affairs but cooperating in the pursuit of common aims and purposes in world affairs. Moreover, these differences may be transitory. In time they may be resolved. Our duty is to see them in perspective against the background of our long association. Of this, at any rate, I am certain: those of us who by grace of the electorate are temporarily in charge of affairs in your country and in mine, we fleeting transient phantoms on the great stage of history, we have no right to sweep aside on this account the friendship that exists between our countries, for that is the legacy of history. It is not ours alone to deal with as we wish. To adapt a famous phrase, it belongs to those who are living, but it also belongs to those who are dead and to those who are yet unborn. We must face the differences, but let us try to see beyond them down the long vista of the future.

I hope – indeed, I am confident – that in another 50 years we shall look back on the differences that exist between us now as matters of historical interest, for as time passes and one generation yields to another, human problems change and fade. Let us remember these truths. Let us resolve to build, not to destroy, and let us remember always that weakness comes from division, strength from unity.

Reproduced from the archive of the late
Harold Macmillan by kind permission of the Trustees
of the Harold Macmillan Book Trust.

This report of Macmillan's speech to the South African
parliament appeared in the *Guardian* on February 4 1960.

PLAIN WORDS TO SOUTH AFRICA
Premier tells why Britain opposes her policies

From our correspondent

Mr Macmillan's speech to the South African Parliament here
today, in which he unexpectedly went out of his way to
emphasise the differences between British and South African
policies in Africa, is hailed locally as a political event of
considerable significance to the Union.

The speech, which was broadcast, clearly took Dr Verwoerd
by surprise, and when the Union Premier stood up to thank
Mr Macmillan, he appeared less confident and assertive than
he usually is. In nationalist quarters, hope had been expressed
that Mr Macmillan would say something which could be
interpreted as indicating that the Union's position in the
Commonwealth would be unaffected by a change in her
Constitution to a republic.

Instead they got a blunt admission that there were radical
differences between British and Union race policies in Africa,
and a declaration that Britain had faith in her own view-
point and proposed to stick to it.

The passage in Mr Macmillan's speech that has created

the greatest impression among parliamentarians is: 'As a fellow member of the Commonwealth we have always tried to give South Africa our support and encouragement, but I hope you will not mind my saying frankly that there are some aspects of your policies which make it impossible for us to do this without being false to our own deep convictions about the political destinies of free men to which, in our territories, we are trying to give effect.'

A sense of drama

There was a sense of drama – the drama of two Commonwealth Premiers differing on the same platform in public when Dr Verwoerd said: 'On an occasion like this, when we can be perfectly frank, we can say we differ from you. There may be very great dangers inherent in that the very objects for which you are aiming may be defeated.'

The speeches of both Mr Macmillan and Dr Verwoerd are published verbatim in all the afternoon newspapers. The South African press also publishes strong criticisms from Britain of the Macmillan tour of the Union on the score that he has been too confined and has not been permitted to meet with African, Indian and Coloured leaders. Today he had private talks with Opposition leaders in parliament, including Sir de Villiers Graaff (United party), Dr Jan Steytler (Progressive), and yesterday he met Mrs Margaret Ballinger (Liberal).

Justice also for whites: Dr Verwoerd's reply

In his short speech proposing a vote of thanks to Mr Macmillan, Dr Verwoerd, the South African Premier, said: 'I am pleased you were frank. We are people who are capable of listening with great pleasure to what other people have to say to us, even if we differ.' Justice had to be done to all. There must not only be justice to the black man in Africa, but also to the white man,' he said amid applause. 'We see ourselves as part of the Western world – a true white state in Southern Africa, with a possibility of granting a full future to the black man in our midst.'

Mr Macmillan's visit showed that 'you wish to be our friend as we wish to be yours'.

It showed that there existed now, and would continue to exist, the best friendship and cooperation on those things such as the economic field, where the two countries could operate.

'Major objectives' endorsed

Dr Verwoerd added: 'I do not find fault with the major objects you have in view. South Africa has the same objects – peace, to which you have made a very considerable contribution and for which I also wish to thank you today, and the survival of Western ideas of civilisation. You have thrown in your weight on the side of the Western nations – we are with you there.'

Dr Verwoerd said: 'We are whites but we are in Africa.

We believe that places on us a special duty. I assure you that in the Christian philosophy, which you endorse, we find a philosophy which we must follow.'

Ask not what your
country can do for you

JOHN F KENNEDY
January 20 1961

This speech was delivered by
John F Kennedy at his inauguration
in Washington on January 20 1961.

Ted Sorensen

Ted Sorensen is an author and lawyer. He was
special counsel and adviser to John F Kennedy
and was his primary speechwriter.

John F Kennedy's inaugural address – delivered on a bitterly
cold, snow-laden January 20 1961 – was a joint effort, like
most of his major speeches during the previous eight years
of our collaboration, and was the culmination of his long
uphill quest for the presidency. He won that prize in the
previous November's election with the narrowest popular
vote margin. He was the first Catholic to be entrusted with
the presidency and, at 43, was the youngest ever elected. The
inaugural address, in my view, was not Kennedy's best speech.
That honour goes to his American University commencement address, June 10 1963, in which he called, as no
American president or other western leader had ever called,
for a re-examination of the Cold War, a re-examination of

our country's relations with Russia, and a re-examination of the meaning of peace. Before that challenge to his country-men was out, the new president unilaterally declared a suspension of American nuclear testing in the atmosphere.

The inaugural may not even have been Kennedy's most important speech historically, in terms of its impact on our planet. That description belongs to his televised address of October 22 1962, which revealed to the world the sudden and theretofore secret presence of Soviet intermediate-range nuclear missiles on Cuba, merely 90 miles from US shores, and firmly set forth his response, formulated over the previous week, seeking the peaceful withdrawal of those missiles (which, six grim days later, he achieved without firing a shot).

Nevertheless, Kennedy's inaugural address was world-changing, heralding the commencement of a new American administration and foreign policy determined upon a peaceful victory in the west's long cold war struggle with the Soviet Union over the world's future direction. JFK had five personal objectives embarking upon that speech, and achieved them all.

1. Recognising that his youthfulness had caused doubts among such venerable allied leaders as Harold Macmillan, Charles de Gaulle and Konrad Adenauer, he wanted to convey his seriousness of purpose and knowledgeable grasp of global issues.

2. Speaking at the height of the Cold War, he wanted to make clear to Soviet chairman Nikita Khrushchev that America's new leader preferred not a 'hot war' but genuine peace, negotiations and cooperation; that, while standing

firm against any armed encroachment on freedom, he was seeking to tone down Cold War rancour and tensions.

3. He wanted to win more friends for the United States and the west among the neutral governments of the third world by stressing his concern for global poverty as well as his opposition to dictatorship.

4. Long a student of history, and with a clear sense of his own place in it, he wanted his first speech as president to fit the moment – to be eloquent, shorter than most, using elevated language to summon the American people to the challenges, sacrifices and discipline that he knew lay ahead.

5. Finally, recognising that both his narrow margin of and his party's loss of seats in the House of Representatives would create serious obstacles to his governance, he wanted no trace of political partisanship in the speech. He thus avoided virtually all domestic issues as inherently divisive. He also wanted to stress that his age – far from representing an excuse to shrink from responsibility – represented instead the 'passing of the torch' of leadership to a new generation ready to assume great responsibilities.

He sounded themes too little heard since his untimely death some 1,000 days later: that 'civility is not a sign of weakness'; that the United Nations is 'our last best hope'; that the purpose of acquiring superiority in armaments was to be certain 'beyond doubt that they will never be employed'; and that the United States sought not to act alone but to join with its adversaries as well as its allies in a 'grand and global alliance' against the 'common enemies of man: tyranny, poverty, disease, and war itself'. Those who thought his vow to 'pay any price, bear any burden ... oppose any foe' was a fierce cry of the Cold War failed to read those other passages.

In working on the speech, he did not ask me to 'clear' the draft with the military joint chiefs of staff or the leaders of both parties in Congress. It was a statement of core values – his and the nation's at that time – that he very much believed needed to be conveyed. They still need to be conveyed, more now than 46 years ago. Where is the leader wise and courageous enough to convey them?

Ask not what your country can do for you

JOHN F KENNEDY
January 20 1961

Vice-president Johnson, Mr Speaker, Mr Chief Justice, President Eisenhower, Vice-president Nixon, President Truman, reverend clergy, fellow citizens: We observe today not a victory of party, but a celebration of freedom – symbolising an end, as well as a beginning – signifying renewal, as well as change. For I have sworn before you and almighty God the same solemn oath our forebears prescribed nearly a century and three-quarters ago.

The world is very different now. For man holds in his mortal hands the power to abolish all forms of human poverty and all forms of human life. And yet the same revolutionary beliefs for which our forebears fought are still at issue around the globe – the belief that the rights of man come not from the generosity of the state, but from the hand of God.

We dare not forget today that we are the heirs of that first revolution. Let the word go forth from this time and place, to friend and foe alike, that the torch has been passed to a new generation of Americans – born in this century, tempered by war, disciplined by a hard and bitter peace, proud of our ancient heritage, and unwilling to witness or permit the slow undoing of those human rights to which this nation has always been committed, and to which we are committed today at home and around the world. Let every nation know, whether it wishes us well or ill, that we shall pay any price, bear any burden, meet any hardship, support any friend, oppose any foe, to assure the survival and the success of liberty.

This much we pledge – and more. To those old allies whose cultural and spiritual origins we share, we pledge the loyalty of faithful friends. United, there is little we cannot do in a host of cooperative ventures. Divided, there is little we can do – for we dare not meet a powerful challenge at odds and split asunder.

To those new states whom we welcome to the ranks of the free, we pledge our word that one form of colonial control shall not have passed away merely to be replaced by a far more iron tyranny. We shall not always expect to find them supporting our view. But we shall always hope to find them strongly supporting their own freedom – and to remember that, in the past, those who foolishly sought power by riding the back of the tiger ended up inside.

To those people in the huts and villages of half the globe struggling to break the bonds of mass misery, we pledge our best efforts to help them help themselves, for whatever period is required – not because the communists may be doing it, not because we seek their votes, but because it is right. If a free society cannot help the many who are poor, it cannot save the few who are rich.

To our sister republics south of our border, we offer a special pledge: to convert our good words into good deeds in a new alliance for progress, to assist free men and free governments in casting off the chains of poverty. But this peaceful revolution of hope cannot become the prey of hostile powers. Let all our neighbours know that we shall join with them to oppose aggression or subversion anywhere in the Americas. And let every other power know that this hemisphere intends to remain the master of its own house.

To that world assembly of sovereign states, the United Nations, our last best hope in an age where the instruments of war have far outpaced the instruments of peace, we renew our pledge of support – to prevent it from becoming merely a forum for invective, to strengthen its shield of the new and the weak, and to enlarge the area in which its writ may run.

Finally, to those nations who would make themselves our adversary, we offer not a pledge but a request: that both sides begin anew the quest for peace, before the dark powers of destruction unleashed by science engulf all humanity in planned or accidental self-destruction. We dare not tempt them with weakness. For only when our arms are sufficient beyond doubt can we be certain beyond doubt that they will never be employed.

But neither can two great and powerful groups of nations

take comfort from our present course – both sides over-burdened by the cost of modern weapons, both rightly alarmed by the steady spread of the deadly atom, yet both racing to alter that uncertain balance of terror that stays the hand of mankind's final war.

So let us begin anew – remembering on both sides that civility is not a sign of weakness, and sincerity is always subject to proof. Let us never negotiate out of fear, but let us never fear to negotiate.

Let both sides explore what problems unite us instead of belabouring those problems which divide us. Let both sides, for the first time, formulate serious and precise proposals for the inspection and control of arms, and bring the absolute power to destroy other nations under the absolute control of all nations. Let both sides seek to invoke the wonders of science instead of its terrors.

Together let us explore the stars, conquer the deserts, eradicate disease, tap the ocean depths, and encourage the arts and commerce. Let both sides unite to heed, in all corners of the earth, the command of Isaiah – to 'undo the heavy burdens, and let the oppressed go free.' And, if a beachhead of cooperation may push back the jungle of suspicion, let both sides join in creating a new endeavour – not a new balance of power, but a new world of law – where the strong are just, and the weak secure, and the peace preserved.

All this will not be finished in the first 100 days. Nor will it be finished in the first 1,000 days, nor in the life of this administration, nor even perhaps in our lifetime on this planet. But let us begin.

In your hands, my fellow citizens, more than mine, will rest the final success or failure of our course. Since this country was founded, each generation of Americans has been summoned to give testimony to its national loyalty. The graves of young Americans who answered the call to service surround the globe. Now the trumpet summons us again – not as a call to bear arms, though arms we need; not as a call to battle, though embattled we are; but a call to bear the burden of a long twilight struggle, year in and year out, 'rejoicing in hope, patient in tribulation', a struggle against the common enemies of man: tyranny, poverty, disease, and war itself.

Can we forge against these enemies a grand and global alliance, north and south, east and west, that can assure a more fruitful life for all mankind? Will you join in that historic effort?

In the long history of the world, only a few generations have been granted the role of defending freedom in its hour of maximum danger. I do not shrink from this responsibility – I welcome it.

I do not believe that any of us would exchange places with any other people or any other generation. The energy, the faith, the devotion which we bring to this endeavour will light our country and all who serve it. And the glow from that fire can truly light the world.

And so, my fellow Americans, ask not what your country

can do for you; ask what you can do for your country. My fellow citizens of the world, ask not what America will do for you, but what, together, we can do for the freedom of man.

Finally, whether you are citizens of America or citizens of the world, ask of us here the same high standards of strength and sacrifice which we ask of you. With a good conscience our only sure reward, with history the final judge of our deeds, let us go forth to lead the land we love, asking His blessing and His help, but knowing that here on earth, God's work must truly be our own.

These articles covering Kennedy's inauguration
ran in the *Guardian* on January 21 1961.
They have been edited and abridged.

MR KENNEDY DONS THE PURPLE
Thirty-fifth President of the United States

From Max Freedman, Washington

Mr John Fitzgerald Kennedy became the thirty-fifth President
of the United States at noon today in a ceremony whose
mingled simplicity and solemnity lost none of its grandeur
because the city was numbed by a storm that left six inches
of snow on the main streets and chilled the festive gaiety of
Inaugural Day.

From the standpoint of the weather it was the worst day
since President Taft took the oath of office in 1909 after a
blizzard. But no one seemed to regard the storm as an omen
of bad luck for the coming years.

Mr Kennedy himself, in an address of solemn dedication
exalted by the pageantry of great phrasing, greeted the challenge of the unknown future by declaring that he would
never shrink from responsibility and would always welcome
it. Rarely has the anthem of courage been sounded so reso-
nantly or so bravely in recent years.

President Kennedy will give his views on specific problems

when he sends his first State of the Union message to Congress. In his inaugural address he was content to define the spirit and purpose of his Administration.

Peace with justice

It will be a spirit of leadership to sustain the purpose of the free world in seeking peace with justice. The President said the United States should never negotiate with the Communist world out of fear, but it should never fear to negotiate.

He spoke not only as the supreme leader of the American people in a period of danger but also as the central guardian of the hopes of free nations everywhere, whether in the old lands of Europe or in the new homes of liberty in Asia and Africa. He knew that he stood on fortune's crowning slope, the pillar of a people's hope, the centre of a world's desire.

Old and new

The members of the Eisenhower Cabinet shared places on the platform with the new Cabinet. With them were the members of the House and Senate, Chief Justice Warren, the governors of 50 States, the joint Chiefs of Staff and the Ambassadors of foreign countries who testify by their abundant company to this country's leadership in world affairs.

The graceful transition between the old and the new reached its climax as a special committee, amid reverberant cheers, escorted Mr Eisenhower and Mr Nixon to the platform. After a suitable pause the committee brought Mr Kennedy and Mr Johnson to the inaugural platform.

The stately figure of Chief Justice Warren seemed to acquire an added distinction as his vibrant voice intoned the consecrated words which brought President Kennedy to the exalted duties of his office, and the austere voices of four religious faiths uttered their consolation and their challenge as the President listened with grave and almost anxious attention. There were Cardinal Cushing of Boston, Archbishop Jakovos of the Greek Orthodox Church, the Rev John Barclay of the Central Church in Austin, Texas, and Rabbi Nelson Glueck.

Nor did the light fall from distant ramparts alone on the spires of the human spirit. A message of inspiration came in the form of the incomparable voice of Miss Marian Anderson which lifted in solemn song. The unfaltering faith that freedom will always be domiciled in America shone through in one of Mr Robert Frost's quiet, immortal poems, which he read with artless beauty.

The big parade

The happy crowds, in their thousands in spite of the cold, rejoiced in the music of the US Marine Band; and only a darkened spirit could find something incongruous in an inaugural ceremony that began with a prayer and ended with a parade, whose splendid diversity, rolled through this city for three hours.

But the last thought was neither of rejoicing nor of fun. It was of the man, no longer young, unbowed by defeat, unafraid of responsibility, and eager for greatness.

He can achieve that greatness only as his country serves causes greater than its own power and as large as the hopes of mankind.

President Kennedy – leading article

'The torch has been passed to a new generation of Americans.' These words set the tone of President Kennedy's brave and dignified inaugural address. He has already shown himself to be a tough-minded politician. Yesterday he showed that he also possesses the sense of history and his own place in it, without which creative leadership is impossible. He offered no panaceas, no easy solutions to the problems that lie ahead. He offered only 'a long twilight struggle' and the inspiring example of a man dedicating himself to great responsibilities.

Global audience

His address was directed almost as much to the outside world as it was to the American people themselves. This was inevitable and proper. The greatest challenges which President Kennedy faces lie in the field of foreign affairs, and it is by his handling of these that he will be judged. But that was not the only reason for his concern with them. The nation which began its life determined to avoid the entanglements of the Old World has become the leader of a coalition of nations; and its most pressing problems cannot be solved without the co-operation of its allies. Immediately after the Second World War, when Europe was devastated and bankrupt, only the United States could give leadership – and she had to give it almost alone. That is no longer true, although many Europeans behave as though it were. Now, and for the foreseeable future, her problems are our problems; and it is for us to respond to President Kennedy's call for energy, courage, and responsibility.

Priorities

President Kennedy, as is customary on such occasions, confined himself to generalities. Nevertheless, he made clear what he considers to be the most urgent tasks. The first, and in some respects the most important, is to preserve the cohesion of the Western Alliance. The second is to pursue disarmament and peace. The third is to speed up the economic development of the poor nations and preserve the independence of the uncommitted world. These tasks cannot be approached in isolation. For the problems that lie behind them are inextricably linked. Yet the solutions are not always compatible.

The cohesion of the Alliance cannot be secured without far-reaching reforms. Unless these reforms are accompanied by a change in its military dispositions, and an increased readiness to make reasonable concessions to the Soviet bloc, disarmament and peace cannot be pursued with any success. Unless the Alliance is united, sufficient economic aid will not be forthcoming, for a greater share of the burden will have to be borne by Western Europe. Yet if the unity of the Alliance is put first, the new Administration may find it hard to pay the price of goodwill in the uncommitted world: there may be times, for example, when it has to choose between offending the Colonial Powers and offending the newly independent former Colonies.

Heir of a revolution

President Kennedy's best hope is to act in the spirit of the passage in his inaugural speech, in which he reminded his listeners that America is the heir of a revolution. This may mean offending conservative politicians in Europe, but it will pay dividends in the uncommitted world. He should throw American weight behind the proposals tentatively put forward by the Labour Party in this country for a reform of NATO. He should secure the withdrawal of nuclear weapons from the front line in Germany and do all he can to persuade the Germans to agree. He should recognise that the present status of West Berlin cannot last for ever. President Kennedy said nothing about domestic politics. But the new Administration also faces critical domestic battles.

The most important, perhaps, lie in the relations between the new Administration and Congress. President Kennedy has a far-reaching programme to enact; and although the men who control Congress belong to his party, he cannot be sure that they will support his programme.

So far the signs are propitious. President Kennedy has shown an excellent grasp of the mechanics of American politics. He seems determined to make sure that key committees are controlled by his supporters; and shows no disposition to forgive those conservative Southerners who failed to give him wholehearted support during the election. Even so, victory will not be easy.

I have a dream

MARTIN LUTHER KING
August 28 1963

This speech was delivered by
Martin Luther King on August 28 1963
at the Lincoln Memorial, Washington.

Gary Younge

Gary Younge is a *Guardian* columnist. An earlier
version of this article appeared in the *Guardian* on
the 40th anniversary of the speech.

Like all great oratory its brilliance was in its simplicity. Like
all great speeches it understood its audience. And like all
great performances it owed as much to delivery as content.
But it stands out because it was both timely in its message
and timeless in its appeal. Martin Luther King's 'I have a
dream' is still pertinent, even though many of its immediate
demands have been met, and it is still relevant, beyond
America's borders and the context that it addressed. Yet, if
President John Kennedy had had his way, it would never
have been delivered. And if King had been left to his own
devices it might have been forgotten.

On June 22 1963, Kennedy met civil rights leaders. A
month before, segregationists in Alabama had turned dogs

on black teenagers. Even as the president stood on a balcony in divided Berlin demanding freedom in eastern Europe, he could not secure it for black people at home. America's racial politics had become an embarrassment. Plans for the August march were already under way. Kennedy, whose civil rights bill faced a tough ride through Congress, pleaded with the leaders to call it off, arguing 'We want success in Congress. Not just a big show at the Capitol.' 'It may seem ill-timed,' said King. 'Frankly, I have never engaged in a direct action ... that did not seem ill-timed.' The march went ahead. Kennedy decided that he would co-opt what he could not cancel, and declared his support.

The prospect of black protesters terrified Washington's white elite, and it is striking that the contemporary *Guardian* report of the march, in which King's speech was not mentioned, does refer to many police and marshals being present (see page 220). Although the Pentagon put 19,000 troops on standby, of the quarter of a million people who turned up, only four – all of them white – were arrested. It was a balmy day, and familiar faces in the crowd included Charlton Heston, Sammy Davis Jr and Marlon Brando. King was the final speaker and everything in his speech, from the cadence of his delivery to the lyrical repetition of its most vital refrains ('I have a dream' or 'Let freedom ring'), drew on the religious traditions of black American politics that merge the pulpit with the podium. It was a basic message made beautiful by his mastery of metaphor. Words to him were like stone to a skilled sculptor, raw material which he deftly chiselled away to shape and define something of aesthetic, as well as practical, value. King had started to wind up the speech, without what has become the signature passage, when the singer Mahalia Jackson, standing nearby, encouraged him to go on. When he began to tell the crowd, 'Go back to Mississippi, go back to Alabama,' she urged him, 'Tell them about your dream, Martin.'

King went on to draw upon a version of a speech he had made many times before. But on the steps of the Lincoln Memorial, the substance of the words rose to the symbolism of the occasion. In a nation apprehensive about its global status, the speech was a precision strike. Starting with Abraham Lincoln and ending with 'a dream deeply rooted in the American dream', it challenged segregation but left intact almost everything else that white America held dear. Not surprisingly, blacks and whites understood the speech differently. A poll soon afterwards showed only 3% of blacks and 74% of whites believed that 'negroes [were] moving too fast'. Given that the inequality which sparked the march still exists, it is not surprising differences in interpretation continue. Many white Americans saw the civil-rights legislation, passed two years later, as drawing a line under racial inequality. Not only would they resist demands to address the legacy of segregation through affirmative action, they would do so with King's own words, insisting that job candidates 'not be judged by the colour of their skin but by the content of their character'.

But King had stated clearly that '1963 is not an end but

a beginning'. In an interview just before he died he explained that overcoming economic deprivation was essential to making the dream a reality. His wish that 'the sons of former slaves and the sons of former slave owners will be able to sit down together at the table of brotherhood' was sincere, but not the whole story. Integration had won African-Americans the right to eat in any restaurant. Only equality could ensure that they could pay the bill. Integration was not an end in itself but the means towards that still-elusive goal. In King's words, black Americans had 'come to our nation's capital to cash a cheque ... that will give [them] the riches of freedom'. They are still waiting for America to honour it.

I have a dream

MARTIN LUTHER KING
August 28 1963

I am happy to join with you today in what will go down in history as the greatest demonstration for freedom in the history of our nation.

Five score years ago, a great American, in whose symbolic shadow we stand today, signed the Emancipation Proclamation. This momentous decree came as a great beacon-light of hope to millions of negro slaves, who had been seared in the flames of withering injustice. It came as a joyous daybreak to end the long night of their captivity. But one hundred years later, the negro still is not free. One hundred years later, the life of the negro is still sadly crippled by the manacle of segregation and the chains of discrimination.

One hundred years later, the negro lives on a lonely island of poverty in the midst of a vast ocean of material prosperity. One hundred years later, the negro is still languished in the corners of American society and finds himself an exile in his own land. So we've come here today to dramatise a shameful condition.

In a sense, we've come to our nation's capital to cash a cheque. When the architects of our republic wrote the magnificent words of the constitution and the Declaration of Independence, they were signing a promissory note to which every American was to fall heir.

This note was a promise that all men – yes, black men as well as white men – would be guaranteed the inalienable rights of life, liberty, and the pursuit of happiness.

It is obvious today that America has defaulted on this promissory note in so far as her citizens of colour are concerned. Instead of honouring this sacred obligation, America has given the negro people a bad cheque, a cheque which has come back marked 'insufficient funds'.

But we refuse to believe that the bank of justice is bankrupt. We refuse to believe that there are insufficient funds in the great vaults of opportunity of this nation. So we have come to cash this cheque, a cheque that will give us upon demand the riches of freedom and the security of justice.

We have also come to this hallowed spot to remind America of the fierce urgency of now. This is no time to engage in the luxury of cooling off or to take the tranquillising drug of gradualism.

Now is the time to make real the promises of democracy.

Now is the time to rise from the dark and desolate valley of segregation to the sunlit path of racial justice.

Now is the time to lift our nation from the quicksands of racial injustice to the solid rock of brotherhood.

Now is the time to make justice a reality for all of God's children.

It would be fatal for the nation to overlook the urgency of the moment. This sweltering summer of the negro's legitimate discontent will not pass until there is an invigorating autumn of freedom and equality. Nineteen sixty-three is not an end but a beginning.

Those who hope that the negro needed to blow off steam and will now be content will have a rude awakening if the nation returns to business as usual. There will be neither rest nor tranquillity in America until the negro is granted his citizenship rights. The whirlwinds of revolt will continue to shake the foundations of our nation until the bright day of justice emerges.

But there is something that I must say to my people who stand on the warm threshold which leads into the palace of justice. In the process of gaining our rightful place we must not be guilty of wrongful deeds.

Let us not seek to satisfy our thirst for freedom by drinking from the cup of bitterness and hatred. We must forever conduct our struggle on the high plane of dignity and discipline. We must not allow our creative protest to degenerate into physical violence. Again and again we must rise to the majestic heights of meeting physical force with soul force.

The marvellous new militancy which has engulfed the negro community must not lead us to a distrust of all white people, for many of our white brothers, as evidenced by their presence here today, have come to realise that their destiny is tied up with our destiny, and their freedom is inextricably bound to our freedom. We cannot walk alone.

And as we walk, we must make the pledge that we shall always march ahead. We cannot turn back. There are those who are asking the devotees of civil rights, 'When will you be satisfied?' We can never be satisfied as long as the negro is the victim of the unspeakable horrors of police brutality.

We can never be satisfied as long as our bodies, heavy with the fatigue of travel, cannot gain lodging in the motels of the highways and the hotels of the cities.

We cannot be satisfied as long as the negro's basic mobility is from a smaller ghetto to a larger one.

We can never be satisfied as long as our children are stripped of their selfhood and robbed of their dignity by signs stating 'For whites only'.

We cannot be satisfied as long as a negro in Mississippi cannot vote and a negro in New York believes he has nothing for which to vote.

No, no we are not satisfied, and we will not be satisfied until justice rolls down like waters and righteousness like a mighty stream.

I am not unmindful that some of you have come here out of great trials and tribulations. Some of you have come fresh from narrow jail cells. Some of you have come from areas where your quest for freedom left you battered by the storms of persecution and staggered by the winds of police brutality.

You have been the veterans of creative suffering. Continue to work with the faith that unearned suffering is redemptive.

Go back to Mississippi, go back to Alabama, go back to South Carolina, go back to Georgia, go back to Louisiana, go back to the slums and ghettos of our northern cities, knowing that somehow this situation can and will be changed.

Let us not wallow in the valley of despair. I say to you today, my friends, so even though we face the difficulties of today and tomorrow. I still have a dream. It is a dream deeply rooted in the American dream.

I have a dream that one day this nation will rise up and live out the true meaning of its creed: 'We hold these truths to be self-evident that all men are created equal.'

I have a dream that one day, on the red hills of Georgia, the sons of former slaves and the sons of former slave owners will be able to sit down together at the table of brotherhood.

I have a dream that one day even the state of Mississippi, a state sweltering with the heat of injustice, sweltering with the heat of oppression will be transformed into an oasis of freedom and justice.

I have a dream that my four little children will one day live in a nation where they will not be judged by the colour of their skin but by the content of their character.

I have a dream today.

I have a dream that one day down in Alabama, with its vicious racists, with its governor having his lips dripping with the words of interposition and nullification, one day right down in Alabama, little black boys and black girls will be able to join hands with little white boys and white girls as sisters and brothers.

I have a dream today.

I have a dream that one day every valley shall be exalted, every hill and mountain shall be made low, the rough places will be made plain and the crooked places will be made straight, and the glory of the Lord shall be revealed and all flesh shall see it together.

This is our hope. This is the faith that I go back to the south with. With this faith we will be able to hew out of the mountain of despair a stone of hope.

With this faith we will be able to transform the jangling discords of our nation into a beautiful symphony of brotherhood. With this faith we will be able to work together, to pray together, to struggle together, to go to jail together, to stand up for freedom together, knowing that we will be free one day.

This will be the day, this will be the day when all of God's children will be able to sing with new meaning, 'My country tis of thee, sweet land of liberty, of thee I sing. Land where my fathers died, land of the pilgrim's pride, from every mountainside, let freedom ring!'

And if America is to be a great nation, this must become true. So let freedom ring from the prodigious hilltops of New Hampshire. Let freedom ring from the mighty mountains of New York.

Let freedom ring from the heightening Alleghenies of Pennsylvania.

Let freedom ring from the snowcapped Rockies of Colorado.

Let freedom ring from the curvaceous slopes of California.

But not only that, let freedom ring from Stone Mountain of Georgia.

Let freedom ring from Lookout Mountain of Tennessee.

Let freedom ring from every hill and molehill of Mississippi, from every mountainside.

Let freedom ring.

And when this happens, and when we allow freedom ring, when we let it ring from every village and every hamlet, from every state and every city, we will be able to speed up that day when all of God's children, black men and white men, Jews and Gentiles, Protestants and Catholics, will be able to join hands and sing in the words of the old negro spiritual, 'Free at last, free at last. Thank God Almighty, we are free at last.'

Speech copyright © 1963 Martin Luther King Jr, copyright
renewed 1991 Coretta Scott King. All rights reserved.
Reprinted by arrangement with the Heirs to the Estate of
Martin Luther King Jr, c/o Writers House as agent
for the proprietor, New York, NY.

The original report of the march for jobs and freedom is reproduced below. It did not mention King's speech. But by the time of his murder in 1968, King was revered internationally as a speaker – as the second article shows.

200,000 DEMONSTRATE FOR CIVIL RIGHTS
Good order maintained in Washington

From Richard Scott, August 29 1963

The Washington march for jobs and freedom – the largest demonstration of its kind the capital has ever seen – has been an outstanding success. The target of 100,000 marchers was in fact doubled.

Police estimate that over 200,000, of whom perhaps nine-tenths were Negro and one-tenth white, marched into the area around the massive memorial to Abraham Lincoln, who signed the emancipation proclamation 100 years ago. They were in holiday mood, and entirely orderly; the majority were young.

The thousands of police and marshals have been primarily occupied with assisting the footsore and the thirsty, lost children, and those who fainted. In all 1,335 people required treatment. Four arrests were made, none involving demonstrators.

The first trickle of people reached the assembly point at about seven o'clock this morning. By ten o'clock there were some 40,000 and by 11:30 the police estimated the crowd had reached the 100,000 mark.

The weather was ideal, the marchers orderly. Washington's infamous humidity was happily lacking. But over-exertion, excitement, and too many hot dogs took their toll. Scores of marchers fainted and were treated in first-aid stations.

Brotherhood of man

The nature of the march was illustrated by a white man in clerical garb and carrying a placard with these words: 'We march together, Protestants – Catholics – Jews, for the dignity and brotherhood of all men under God.' Other placards said: 'No US dough to help Jim Crow grow'; 'We demand equal rights now'; 'We demand an FE (fair employment) law now'; 'We demand an end to police brutality now.'

Every sort and condition of humanity was represented – well-dressed young men and women, a few women in slacks, many clergymen, an occasional white beatnik in beard and jeans, a Negro in a wheelchair holding a placard reading 'Help my people.' The folk-singer Odetta led a huge audience in an emotional version of 'Where I Stand.' Earlier this morning the leaders of the 10 organisations which sponsored the march went to Capitol Hill to meet Democratic and Republican leaders of Congress and, after the march was over, President Kennedy.

In turn, the leaders of the main organisations which have sponsored the march delivered brief addresses. Their theme, like that on the placards carried by the marchers, was that equal rights in full must be granted NOW to all American citizens regardless of their race or religion. They were, with one exception, uninflammatory, sober statements.

President Kennedy said that he was impressed with the deep fervour and the quiet dignity of the demonstrators.

King this side of Jordan – By Jonathan Steele
April 6 1968

'He was the first Negro minister whom I have ever heard who can reduce the Negro problem to a spiritual matter and yet inspire the people to seek a solution on this side of the Jordan, not in life after death.' So wrote the Negro author, Louis Lomax, catching the crucial spark that made Martin Luther King, Jr stand out from his fellow ministers in the South, and step into the ranks of the world's martyrs.

To anyone who was ever there when King spoke, the experience was unforgettable. A small man, barely five foot seven, he dominated the pulpit or the podium. In a slow but sonorous voice, the biblical cadences rolled out, and the crowd would sway with them, and punctuate them with the answering calls that are such a feature of Negro churches. And the church doors would open and the crowd would surge out into the hot and dusty Southern street, and down to the court house or the city hall with its petitions, its banners and its faith that change was on the way.

An ideal for which
I am prepared to die

NELSON MANDELA
April 20 1964

This is an edited and abridged version of
Nelson Mandela's statement from the dock
at the opening of his trial on charges of sabotage,
Supreme court of South Africa, Pretoria, April 20 1964.

For ease of reading, individual excisions are not marked,
nor is it indicated when the case of a letter changes
due to the deletion of part of a sentence.

The full text is available at the ANC's website:
www.anc.org.za/ancdocs/history/rivonia.html

FW de Klerk

FW de Klerk was president of South Africa, 1989–1994.
In 1993 he was, with Nelson Mandela, the joint
recipient of the Nobel peace prize.

Nelson Mandela's 1964 speech – with its dignified exposition of the tribulations of black South Africans under apartheid – was received with indifference by the National party government. His reasoned explanation of how the African National Congress came to embark on its armed struggle was seized on as vindication for the decision to crack down; his advancement of non-racial socialist democracy was regarded as a mortal threat to the Afrikaner nation. Today the injustice of apartheid is admitted by most of those who supported the National party at the time. I, in my capacity as National party leader, offered a profound apology before the Truth and Reconciliation Commission.

As Mandela correctly observed, the main concern of white

South Africans in 1964 was that universal franchise would extinguish self-determination for Afrikaners and whites more broadly. It was feared that it would lead to one man, one vote, one time – as was happening in many newly independent nations. And there was concern about the influence of the Communist party on the ANC.

Fortunately, Nelson Mandela did not die for his ideals. After 27 years in prison, he lived to lead his people to the non-racial democracy that he had envisioned – surely one of the most inspiring political sagas of any age. I was privileged to have been able to initiate the transformation – and to lead my own constituency into the new South Africa. By that time many of the injustices of which Mandela had complained had been partially alleviated: the hated pass laws had been scrapped; trade union rights had been granted; and most apartheid laws had been repealed. By 1990, the annual number of black matriculants had grown from the 362 reported by Mandela to more than 110,000. Yet after much internal debate we realised that apartheid could not be reformed, for it was morally wrong. It had to be dismantled entirely and replaced with a non-racial democracy. This we achieved after four years of tortuous negotiation.

In the final analysis, it was not the ANC's armed struggle that led the National party to the negotiating table – nor was it sanctions and international pressure, important though these were. The collapse of global communism was certainly one factor, but the main agents of change were evolutionary social forces during the decades following

Mandela's trial. Millions of black South Africans moved to the cities and improved their living standards and education. By 1989 they were indispensable to the economy. Apartheid was doomed from the moment that young black and white people with the same qualifications began working side by side in the 80s, in banks, shops and factories. White attitudes changed too. In the decades following 1964, a generation of young Afrikaners moved from small farms and working-class jobs to the middle class. They graduated and travelled abroad – and were influenced by global attitudes. They no longer shared the narrow nationalism of their parents and became uncomfortable with apartheid. By 1989 they were ripe for change.

And so Nelson Mandela's vision was broadly fulfilled. He became the first president of our non-racial democracy and worked tirelessly for reconciliation. The indignity of apartheid has gone. We have enjoyed prolonged economic growth. Tourism is booming. A new black middle class has emerged and South Africa is again a highly respected nation. Yet aspects of Mandela's 1964 vision remain frustrated. Half the black population still live below the poverty line. Crime is at unacceptable levels and 6 million South Africans are HIV positive. Mandela was unfortunately wrong when he said that, 'Political division, based on colour, is entirely artificial and, when it disappears, so will the domination of one colour group by another.' Sadly, political divisions are still based on colour. Whites remain economically privileged, but have virtually no say in the policies by which they are governed. Those policies increasingly – and perhaps understandably – involve affirmative action and wealth redistribution. Many Afrikaners believe they are subject to new forms of racial domination – and 20% of the white population has emigrated.

Despite all this, the new South Africa is a far, far better place than the bleak scene of pervasive repression, discrimination and poverty depicted by Nelson Mandela in his speech. Today, he is universally loved by large majorities of all our communities. I am happy to call him my friend. Much of the vision that he portrayed in his speech has been achieved – but much still remains to be done.

An ideal for which
I am prepared to die

Nelson Mandela
April 20 1964

I am the first accused. I hold a bachelor's degree in arts and practised as an attorney in Johannesburg for a number of years in partnership with Oliver Tambo. I am a convicted prisoner serving five years for leaving the country without a permit and for inciting people to go on strike at the end of May 1961.

At the outset, I want to say that the suggestion that the struggle in South Africa is under the influence of foreigners or communists is wholly incorrect. I have done whatever I did because of my experience in South Africa and my own proudly felt African background, and not because of what any outsider might have said. In my youth in the Transkei I listened to the elders of my tribe telling stories of the old days. Amongst the tales they related to me were those of wars fought by our ancestors in defence of the fatherland. The names of Dingane and Bambata, Hintsa and Makana, Squngthi and Dalasile, Moshoeshoe and Sekhukhuni, were

229

praised as the glory of the entire African nation. I hoped then that life might offer me the opportunity to serve my people and make my own humble contribution to their freedom struggle.

Some of the things so far told to the court are true and some are untrue. I do not, however, deny that I planned sabotage. I did not plan it in a spirit of recklessness, nor because I have any love of violence. I planned it as a result of a calm and sober assessment of the political situation that had arisen after many years of tyranny, exploitation, and oppression of my people by the whites.

I admit immediately that I was one of the persons who helped to form Umkhonto we Sizwe. I deny that Umkhonto was responsible for a number of acts which clearly fell outside the policy of the organisation, and which have been charged in the indictment against us. I, and the others who started the organisation, felt that without violence there would be no way open to the African people to succeed in their struggle against the principle of white supremacy. All lawful modes of expressing opposition to this principle had been closed by legislation, and we were placed in a position in which we had either to accept a permanent state of inferiority, or to defy the government. We chose to defy the law.

We first broke the law in a way which avoided any recourse to violence; when this form was legislated against, and then the government resorted to a show of force to crush opposition to its policies, only then did we decide to answer violence with violence.

The African National Congress was formed in 1912 to defend the rights of the African people, which had been seriously curtailed. For 37 years – that is, until 1949 – it adhered strictly to a constitutional struggle. But white governments remained unmoved, and the rights of Africans became less instead of becoming greater. Even after 1949, the ANC remained determined to avoid violence. At this time, however, the decision was taken to protest against apartheid by peaceful, but unlawful, demonstrations. More than 8,500 people went to jail. Yet there was not a single instance of violence. I and 19 colleagues were convicted for organising the campaign, but our sentences were suspended mainly because the judge found that discipline and non-violence had been stressed throughout.

During the defiance campaign, the Public Safety Act and the Criminal Law Amendment Act were passed. These provided harsher penalties for protests against [the] laws. Despite this, the protests continued and the ANC adhered to its policy of non-violence. In 1956, 156 leading members of the Congress Alliance, including myself, were arrested. The non-violent policy of the ANC was put in issue by the state, but when the court gave judgment some five years later, it found that the ANC did not have a policy of violence.

In 1960 there was the shooting at Sharpeville, which resulted in the declaration of the ANC as an unlawful organisation. My colleagues and I, after careful consideration, decided that we would not obey this decree. The African people were not part of the government and did not make the laws by which they were governed. We believed in the words of the Universal Declaration of Human Rights, that 'the will of the people shall be the basis of authority of the government', and for us to accept the banning was equivalent to accepting the silencing of the Africans for all time. The ANC refused to dissolve, but instead went underground.

In 1960 the government held a referendum which led to the establishment of the republic. Africans, who constituted approximately 70% of the population, were not entitled to vote, and were not even consulted. I undertook to be responsible for organising the national stay-at-home called to coincide with the declaration of the republic. As all strikes by Africans are illegal, the person organising such a strike must avoid arrest. I had to leave my home and family and my practice and go into hiding to avoid arrest. The stay-at-home was to be a peaceful demonstration. Careful instructions were given to avoid any recourse to violence.

The government's answer was to introduce new and harsher laws, to mobilise its armed forces, and to send Saracens, armed vehicles, and soldiers into the townships in a massive show of force designed to intimidate the people. The government had decided to rule by force alone, and this decision was a milestone on the road to Umkhonto. What were we, the leaders of our people, to do? We had no doubt that we had to continue the fight. Anything else would have been abject surrender. Our problem was not whether to fight, but was how to continue the fight.

We of the ANC had always stood for a non-racial

democracy, and we shrank from any action which might drive the races further apart. But the hard facts were that 50 years of non-violence had brought the African people nothing but more and more repressive legislation, and fewer and fewer rights. By this time violence had, in fact, become a feature of the South African political scene.

There had been violence in 1957 when the women of Zeerust were ordered to carry passes; there was violence in 1958 with the enforcement of cattle culling in Sekhukhuneland; there was violence in 1959 when the people of Cato Manor protested against pass raids; there was violence in 1960 when the government attempted to impose Bantu authorities in Pondoland. Each disturbance pointed to the inevitable growth among Africans of the belief that violence was the only way out – it showed that a government which uses force to maintain its rule teaches the oppressed to use force to oppose it.

I came to the conclusion that as violence in this country was inevitable, it would be unrealistic to continue preaching peace and non-violence. This conclusion was not easily arrived at. It was only when all else had failed, when all channels of peaceful protest had been barred to us, that the decision was made to embark on violent forms of political struggle. I can only say that I felt morally obliged to do what I did.

Four forms of violence were possible. There is sabotage, there is guerrilla warfare, there is terrorism, and there is open revolution. We chose to adopt the first. Sabotage did not involve loss of life, and it offered the best hope for future race relations. Bitterness would be kept to a minimum and, if the policy bore fruit, democratic government could become a reality. The initial plan was based on a careful analysis of the political and economic situation of our country. We believed that South Africa depended to a large extent on foreign capital. We felt that planned destruction of power plants, and interference with rail and telephone communications, would scare away capital from the country, thus compelling the voters of the country to reconsider their position. Umkhonto had its first operation on December 16 1961, when government buildings in Johannesburg, Port Elizabeth and Durban were attacked. The selection of targets is proof of the policy to which I have referred. Had we intended to attack life we would have selected targets where people congregated and not empty buildings and power stations.

The whites failed to respond by suggesting change; they responded to our call by suggesting the laager. In contrast, the response of the Africans was one of encouragement. Suddenly there was hope again. People began to speculate on how soon freedom would be obtained.

But we in Umkhonto weighed up the white response with anxiety. The lines were being drawn. The whites and blacks were moving into separate camps, and the prospects of avoiding a civil war were made less. The white newspapers carried reports that sabotage would be punished by death. If this was so, how could we continue to keep Africans away from terrorism?

We felt it our duty to make preparations to use force in order to defend ourselves against force. We decided, therefore to make provision for the possibility of guerrilla warfare. All whites undergo compulsory military training, but no such training was given to Africans. It was in our view essential to build up a nucleus of trained men who would be able to provide the leadership which would be required if guerrilla warfare started.

At this stage it was decided that I should attend the Conference of the Pan-African Freedom Movement which was to be held early in 1962 in Addis Ababa, and after the conference, I would undertake a tour of the African states with a view to obtaining facilities for the training of soldiers. My tour was a success. Wherever I went I met sympathy for our cause and promises of help. All Africa was united against the stand of white South Africa, and even in London I was received with great sympathy by political leaders, such as Mr Gaitskell and Mr Grimond.

I started to make a study of the art of war and revolution and, whilst abroad, underwent a course in military training. If there was to be guerrilla warfare, I wanted to be able to stand and fight with my people and to share the hazards of war with them.

On my return I found that there had been little alteration in the political scene save that the threat of a death penalty for sabotage had now become a fact.

Another of the allegations made by the state is that the aims and objects of the ANC and the Communist party are the same. The creed of the ANC is, and always has been, the creed of African nationalism. It is not the concept of African nationalism expressed in the cry, 'Drive the white man into the sea.' The African nationalism for which the ANC stands is the concept of freedom and fulfilment for the African people in their own land. The most important political document ever adopted by the ANC is the 'freedom charter'. It is by no means a blueprint for a socialist state. It calls for redistribution, but not nationalisation, of land; it provides for nationalisation of mines, banks, and monopoly industry, because big monopolies are owned by one race only, and without such nationalisation racial domination would be perpetuated despite the spread of political power. Under the freedom charter, nationalisation would take place in an economy based on private enterprise.

As far as the Communist party is concerned, and if I understand its policy correctly, it stands for the establishment of a state based on the principles of Marxism. The Communist party sought to emphasise class distinctions whilst the ANC seeks to harmonise them. This is a vital distinction.

It is true that there has often been close cooperation between the ANC and the Communist party. But cooperation is merely proof of a common goal – in this case the removal of white supremacy – and is not proof of a complete community of interests. The history of the world is full of similar examples. Perhaps the most striking is the cooperation between Great Britain, the United States and the Soviet Union in the fight against Hitler. Nobody but Hitler would have dared to suggest that such cooperation turned Churchill or Roosevelt into communists. Theoretical differences amongst those fighting against oppression is a luxury we cannot afford at this stage.

What is more, for many decades communists were the only political group in South Africa prepared to treat Africans as human beings and their equals; who were prepared to eat with us; talk with us, live with us, and work with us. They were the only group which was prepared to work with the Africans for the attainment of political rights and a stake in society. Because of this, there are many Africans who, today, tend to equate freedom with communism. They are supported in this belief by a legislature which brands all exponents of democratic government and African freedom as communists and bans many of them (who are not communists) under the Suppression of Communism Act. Although I have never been a member of the Communist party, I myself have been imprisoned under that act.

I have always regarded myself, in the first place, as an African patriot. Today I am attracted by the idea of a classless society, an attraction which springs in part from Marxist reading and, in part, from my admiration of the structure of early African societies. The land belonged to the tribe. There were no rich or poor and there was no exploitation. We all accept the need for some form of socialism to enable our people to catch up with the advanced countries of this world and to overcome their legacy of extreme poverty. But this does not mean we are Marxists.

I have gained the impression that communists regard the parliamentary system of the West as reactionary. But, on the contrary, I am an admirer. The Magna Carta, the Petition of Right, and the Bill of Rights are documents held in veneration by democrats throughout the world. I have great respect for British institutions, and for the country's system of justice. I regard the British parliament as the most democratic institution in the world, and the impartiality of its judiciary never fails to arouse my admiration. The American Congress, that country's separation of powers, as well as the independence of its judiciary, arouses in me similar sentiments.

I have been influenced in my thinking by both west and east. I should tie myself to no particular system of society other than of socialism. I must leave myself free to borrow the best from the west and from the east.

Our fight is against real, and not imaginary, hardships or, to use the language of the state prosecutor, 'so-called hardships'. Basically, we fight against two features which are the hallmarks of African life in South Africa and which are entrenched by legislation. These features are poverty and lack of human dignity, and we do not need communists or so-called 'agitators' to teach us about these things. South Africa is the richest country in Africa, and could be one of the richest countries in the world. But it is a land of remarkable contrasts. The whites enjoy what may be the highest standard of living in the world, whilst Africans live in poverty and misery. Poverty goes hand in hand with malnutrition and disease. Tuberculosis, pellagra and scurvy bring death and destruction of health.

The complaint of Africans, however, is not only that they are poor and the whites are rich, but that the laws which are made by the whites are designed to preserve this situation. There are two ways to break out of poverty. The first is by formal education, and the second is by the worker acquiring a greater skill at his work and thus higher wages. As far as Africans are concerned, both these avenues of advancement are deliberately curtailed by legislation.

The government has always sought to hamper Africans in their search for education. There is compulsory education for all white children at virtually no cost to their parents, be they rich or poor. African children, however, generally have to pay more for their schooling than whites.

Approximately 40% of African children in the age group seven to 14 do not attend school. For those who do, the standards are vastly different from those afforded to white children. Only 5,660 African children in the whole of South Africa passed their junior certificate in 1962, and only 362 passed matric.

This is presumably consistent with the policy of Bantu education about which the present prime minister said: 'When I have control of native education I will reform it so that natives will be taught from childhood to realise that equality with Europeans is not for them. People who believe in equality are not desirable teachers for natives. When my department controls native education it will know for what class of higher education a native is fitted, and whether he will have a chance in life to use his knowledge.'

The other main obstacle to the advancement of the African is the industrial colour-bar under which all the better jobs of industry are reserved for whites only. Moreover, Africans who do obtain employment in the unskilled and semi-skilled occupations open to them are not allowed to form trade unions which have recognition. This means that they are denied the right of collective bargaining, which is permitted to the better-paid white workers.

The government answers its critics by saying that Africans in South Africa are better off than the inhabitants of the other countries in Africa. I do not know whether this state-ment is true. But even if it is true, as far as the African people are concerned it is irrelevant.

Our complaint is not that we are poor by comparison with people in other countries, but that we are poor by comparison with the white people in our own country, and that we are prevented by legislation from altering this imbalance.

The lack of human dignity experienced by Africans is the direct result of the policy of white supremacy. White supremacy implies black inferiority. Legislation designed to preserve white supremacy entrenches this notion. Menial tasks in South Africa are invariably performed by Africans.

When anything has to be carried or cleaned the white man will look around for an African to do it for him, whether the African is employed by him or not. Because of this sort of attitude, whites tend to regard Africans as a separate breed. They do not look upon them as people with families of their own; they do not realise that they have emotions – that they fall in love like white people do; that they want to be with their wives and children like white people want to be with theirs; that they want to earn enough money to support their families properly, to feed and clothe them and send them to school. And what 'house-boy' or 'garden-boy' or labourer can ever hope to do this?

Pass laws render any African liable to police surveillance at any time. I doubt whether there is a single African male in South Africa who has not had a brush with the police over his pass. Hundreds and thousands of Africans are thrown into jail each year under pass laws.

Even worse is the fact that pass laws keep husband and wife apart and lead to the breakdown of family life. Poverty and the breakdown of family have secondary effects. Children wander the streets because they have no schools to go to, or no money to enable them to go, or no parents at home to see that they go, because both parents (if there be two) have to work to keep the family alive. This leads to a breakdown in moral standards, to an alarming rise in illegitimacy, and to violence, which erupts not only politically, but everywhere. Life in the townships is dangerous. Not a day goes by without somebody being stabbed or assaulted. And violence is carried out of the townships [into] the white living areas. People are afraid to walk the streets after dark. Housebreakings and robberies are increasing, despite the fact that the death sentence can now be imposed for such offences. Death sentences cannot cure the festering sore.

Africans want to be paid a living wage. Africans want to perform work which they are capable of doing, and not work which the government declares them to be capable of. Africans want to be allowed to live where they obtain work, and not be endorsed out of an area because they were not born there. Africans want to be allowed to own land in places where they work, and not to be obliged to live in rented houses which they can never call their own. Africans want to be part of the general population, and not confined to living in their own ghettoes.

African men want to have their wives and children to live with them where they work, and not be forced into an unnatural existence in men's hostels. African women want to be with their menfolk and not be left permanently widowed in the reserves. Africans want to be allowed out after 11 o'clock at night and not to be confined to their rooms like little children. Africans want to be allowed to travel in their own country and to seek work where they want to and not where the labour bureau tells them to. Africans want a just share in the whole of South Africa; they want security and a stake in society.

Above all, we want equal political rights, because without them our disabilities will be permanent. I know this sounds revolutionary to the whites in this country, because the majority of voters will be Africans. This makes the white man fear democracy. But this fear cannot be allowed to stand in the way of the only solution which will guarantee racial harmony and freedom for all. It is not true that the enfranchisement of all will result in racial domination. Political division, based on colour, is entirely artificial and, when it disappears, so will the domination of one colour group by another. The ANC has spent half a century fighting against racialism. When it triumphs it will not change that policy.

This then is what the ANC is fighting. Their struggle is a truly national one. It is a struggle of the African people, inspired by their own suffering and their own experience. It is a struggle for the right to live. During my lifetime I have dedicated myself to this struggle of the African people. I have fought against white domination, and I have fought against black domination. I have cherished the ideal of a democratic and free society in which all persons live together in harmony and with equal opportunities. It is an ideal which I hope to live for and to achieve. But if needs be, it is an ideal for which I am prepared to die.

Speech copyright © Nelson Mandela Foundation 2007.
Reproduced by kind permission. All rights reserved.

These reports of the trial of Nelson Mandela and other ANC leaders appeared in the *Guardian* in 1964.

MANDELA PLANNED SABOTAGE IN STRUGGLE FOR EMANCIPATION

From our political correspondent

Pretoria, April 21 1964

Two African leaders, Nelson Mandela and Walter Sisulu, told the court trying them here today that their aim was emancipation from white domination, and they had come to regard violence as inevitable.

Mandela, one of nine people charged with sabotage and plotting revolution, said: 'We had either to accept inferiority or fight against it by violence. We chose the latter.' Both men strongly denied they were communists. The charges against Mandela, former leader of the banned African National Congress, and the other accused include sabotage involving nearly 200 incidents.

The case is known here as the 'Rivonia trial,' from the name of the area just north of Johannesburg where several of the accused were arrested in July. The State has said the house was the headquarters of the 'national high command' of 'Umkhonto we Sizwe' (Spear of the Nation), a militant arm allegedly formed by the underground ANC to achieve the overthrow of the Government in 1963.

Mandela spoke for nearly five hours. He said: 'I do not deny that I planned sabotage. I did not do this in a spirit of recklessness. I planned it as a result of a calm and sober assessment.' He said he had practised as a lawyer.

Inevitable

He concluded in June, 1961, that violence was inevitable and that it would be unrealistic for African leaders to continue a non-violent policy when the Government 'met our demands with violence'.

He said: 'This decision was not easily made. The decision was made to embark on violent forms of struggle. I felt morally obliged to do what I did.'

The ANC was committed not to undertake violence, but was prepared to depart from its policy to the extent that it would no longer disapprove of properly controlled sabotage. The choice of sabotage was made because it would not involve loss of life.

Mandela said he had dedicated his life to end white domination – 'It is an idea [sic] I hope to live and see realised, but it is an idea [sic] for which I am prepared to die.'

The hearing was adjourned till tomorrow. – *Reuter*

Life terms all round in Mandela trial
Pretoria, June 13 1964

Nelson Mandela smiled and gave the thumbs-up sign as he was driven away to life imprisonment today, but was unable to catch a final glimpse of his wife and four-year-old daughter standing forlornly on the corner of the street.

The former leader of the banned African National Congress and the seven other men convicted of sabotage and plotting violent revolution peered eagerly through the steel mesh of the sand-coloured prison lorry as it swept them from the gloom of the Palace of Justice here into bright sunshine. It drove to an unnamed prison, where they will begin their life terms.

Crowds, several thousand strong and dominated by whites, stood for hours in the square facing the Palace of Justice before Mr Justice Quartus de Wet, Judge-President of the Transvaal, sentenced all eight accused to life imprisonment.

The judge told them the crime on which they had been found guilty was 'in essence one of high treason.' He paused in the heavy silence of the Victorian court room, and then added: 'But the State has decided not to treat the crime in this form.'

He said that allowing for this, 'I have decided not to impose the supreme penalty.' But that was the only leniency he could show.

The lady's not for turning

MARGARET THATCHER
October 10 1980

This speech was delivered to the Conservative party
conference in Brighton on October 10 1980.

Simon Jenkins

Simon Jenkins is a *Guardian* columnist and has
written a number of books about Margaret Thatcher
and Thatcherism.

Margaret Thatcher's speech to the 1980 Conservative
conference was that of a woman with her back to the wall.
Seventeen months into office, she was confronting a recession, a sceptical nation, a frightened party and a rebellious
cabinet. Her chancellor had cut the top tax rate while
unemployment rose to 2 million. The cabinet had just been
engaged in a debilitating battle over cuts and, as she recalled,
'my critics within the cabinet first seriously attempted to
frustrate the strategy.' From all sides came pleas to reflate
the economy and soften an image hardening into stony-faced
dogmatism.

Thatcher had come to office in 1979 an unknown quantity.
Her soft-focus femininity and Francis of Assisi quotations

accompanied a bland manifesto mentioning neither monetarism nor privatisation. While emotionally on the right,
Thatcher resisted hawks demanding an instant assault on the
unions. The 1979 and 1980 budgets, with tax concessions, ending
of exchange control and debt repayments, had worried
Thatcher, and she had opposed the immediate tax cut.

None the less there was much of which she was determined to boast. She had forced through a modest reform
of the picketing law. She had taken what can now be seen
as the first steps towards privatising British Aerospace and
British Telecom. She was proud of Michael Heseltine's start
to the sale of council houses, and of her settlement of
Rhodesian independence. Yet for all this, the depths of the
recession now looked like engulfing the government and
condemning her to the same one-term fate of Edward Heath
in 1970–74. Thatcher was wholly sensitive to this danger.
She never failed to mention unemployment in speeches,
calling it 'a human tragedy'. So nervous was she on this
point that, unlike New Labour, she did not dare reform
social benefits. Sickness, unemployment and housing benefit
soared under her rule. Only half-hearted attempts were made
to combat benefit fraud and she refused to countenance coal,
post or rail privatisation, not least as she feared it might
increase unemployment.

Yet of one thing she was adamant, and it echoes through
the speech. There must be no backing away from the defeat
of inflation and no repeat of Heath's 1972 U-turn. The
greatest asset Thatcher brought to Downing Street was

the memory of 1972. The trauma of sitting in the Cabinet room and watching the government being overwhelmed by the miners had her incanting Kipling's lines: 'Let us admit it fairly, as a business people should/ We have had no end of a lesson: it will do us no end of good.'

In 1974, Thatcher's mentor, Sir Keith Joseph, delivered speeches 'repenting' the U-turn in terms that moved Thatcher, first to plead with him to stand against Heath and, when he refused, to stand herself. While she was always a compromiser, she never forgot 1972. Nor could she easily do so, as sitting near her in the Commons was the ghost of that U-turn, the sullen, moody frame of Heath himself. Better to go down fighting than to re-create that great black cloud across the gangway. Hence she rammed the message home time and again: 'Britain had the courage and resolve to sustain discipline for long enough to break through to success' – as Heath had never done. 'Those who urge us to relax the squeeze' – as the Heathites had done – 'are not being kind or compassionate or caring'. All this, she recalled, was 'directed as much to some of my colleagues in the government as it was to politicians of other parties'.

When she came to her peroration, the lines of her speech-writer, Ronnie Miller, baffled many listeners. With U-turn the catchphrase of the moment, Miller punned on the title of the Christopher Fry play, *The Lady's Not for Burning*, a reference that must have been lost on most of the audience: 'You turn if you want to. The lady's not for turning.' It received a roar of applause. Whatever it meant, the idea of an iron lady sure of the medicine the country needed and resolute in administering it became Thatcher's talisman.

The message was never popular except among the die-hard faithful. A year later she faced an even more determined assault from disloyal colleagues, but by then her isolation was equalled by her determination. Irrespective of cabinet or public opinion she would not reverse her anti-inflation policy. After a decade of British leaders to whom policy reversal had become second nature, this was wholly new. Thatcher had many more battles to fight – and the 1982 Falklands war to rescue her for posterity – but 1980 was when she shook off the ghost of 1972 and emerged, loved or hated, as the prime minister she went on to become.

The lady's not for turning

MARGARET THATCHER
October 10 1980

Mr Chairman, ladies and gentlemen, most of my cabinet colleagues have started their speeches of reply by paying very well deserved tributes to their junior ministers. At Number 10, I have no junior ministers. There is just Denis and me, and I could not do without him. I am, however, very fortunate in having a marvellous deputy who is wonderful in all places at all times in all things – Willie Whitelaw.

At our party conference last year I said that the task in which the government were engaged – to change the national attitude of mind – was the most challenging to face any British administration since the war. Challenge is exhilarating. This week we Conservatives have been taking stock, discussing the achievements, the setbacks and the work that lies ahead as we enter our second parliamentary year. As you said, Mr Chairman, our debates have been stimulating and our debates have been constructive. This week has demonstrated that we are a party united in purpose, strategy and resolve. And we actually like one another.

When I am asked for a detailed forecast of what will happen in the coming months or years, I remember Sam Goldwyn's advice: 'Never prophesy, especially about the future.' (*Interruption from the floor*) Never mind, it is wet outside. I expect that they wanted to come in. You cannot blame them; it is always better where the Tories are. And you, and perhaps they, will be looking to me this afternoon for an indication of how the government see the task before us and why we are tackling it the way we are. Before I begin, let me get one thing out of the way.

This week at Brighton we have heard a good deal about last week at Blackpool. I will have a little more to say about that strange assembly later, but for the moment I want to say just this. Because of what happened at that conference, there has been, behind all our deliberations this week, a heightened awareness that now, more than ever, our Conservative government must succeed. We just must, because now there is even more at stake than some had realised.

There are many things to be done to set this nation on the road to recovery, and I do not mean economic recovery alone, but a new independence of spirit and zest for achievement.

It is sometimes said that because of our past, we, as a people, expect too much and set our sights too high. That is not the way I see it. Rather it seems to me that throughout my life in politics our ambitions have steadily shrunk. Our response to disappointment has not been to lengthen our stride but to shorten the distance to be covered. But with confidence in ourselves and in our future, what a nation we could be!

In its first 17 months, this government have laid the foundations for recovery. We have undertaken a heavy load of legislation, a load we do not intend to repeat because we do not share the socialist fantasy that achievement is measured by the number of laws you pass. But there was a formidable barricade of obstacles that we had to sweep aside. For a start, in his first budget Geoffrey Howe began to rest incentives to stimulate the abilities and inventive genius of our people. Prosperity comes not from grand conferences of economists but by countless acts of personal self-confidence and self-reliance.

Under Geoffrey's stewardship, Britain has repaid $3,600m of international debt, debt which had been run up by our predecessors. And we paid quite a lot of it before it was due. In the past 12 months Geoffrey has abolished exchange controls over which British governments have dithered for decades. Our great enterprises are now free to seek opportunities overseas . . . We have made the first crucial changes in trade union law to remove the worst abuses of the closed shop, to restrict picketing to the place of work of the parties in dispute, and to encourage secret ballots.

Jim Prior has carried all these measures through with the support of the vast majority of trade union members . . . British Aerospace will soon be open to private investment. The monopoly of the Post Office and British Telecommunications is being diminished. The barriers to private generation of electricity for sale have been lifted. For the first time nationalised industries and public utilities can be investigated by the monopolies commission – a long overdue reform . . .

Michael Heseltine has given to millions – yes, millions – of council tenants the right to buy their own homes. It was Anthony Eden who chose for us the goal of 'a property-owning democracy'. But for all the time that I have been in public affairs, that has been beyond the reach of so many, who were denied the right to the most basic ownership of all – the homes in which they live. They wanted to buy. Many could afford to buy. But they happened to live under the jurisdiction of a socialist council, which would not sell and did not believe in the independence that comes with ownership. Now Michael Heseltine has given them the chance to turn a dream into reality. And all this and a lot more in 17 months.

The Left continues to refer with relish to the death of capitalism. Well, if this is the death of capitalism, I must say that it is quite a way to go.

But all this will avail us little unless we achieve our prime economic objective – the defeat of inflation. Inflation destroys nations and societies as surely as invading armies do. Inflation is the parent of unemployment. It is the unseen robber of those who have saved. No policy which puts at risk the defeat of inflation – however great its short-term attraction – can be right. Our policy for the defeat of inflation is, in fact, traditional. It existed long before Sterling M3 embellished the Bank of England Quarterly Bulletin, or 'monetarism' became a convenient term of political invective.

But some people talk as if control of the money supply was a revolutionary policy. Yet it was an essential condition for the recovery of much of continental Europe. Those countries knew what was required for economic stability. Previously, they had lived through rampant inflation; they knew that it led to suit-case money, massive unemployment and the breakdown of society itself. They determined never to go that way again.

Today, after many years of monetary self-discipline, they have stable, prosperous economies better able than ours to withstand the buffeting of world recession. So at inter-national conferences to discuss economic affairs, many of my fellow heads of government find our policies not strange, unusual or revolutionary, but normal, sound and honest. And that is what they are. Their only question is: 'Has Britain the courage and resolve to sustain the discipline for long enough to break through to success?'

Yes, Mr Chairman, we have, and we shall. This govern-ment are determined to stay with the policy and see it through to its conclusion. That is what marks this administration as one of the truly radical ministries of postwar Britain. Inflation is falling and should continue to fall.

Meanwhile, we are not heedless of the hardships and worries that accompany the conquest of inflation. Foremost among these is unemployment. Today our country has more than 2 million unemployed.

Now you can try to soften that figure in a dozen ways. You can point out – and it is quite legitimate to do so – that 2 million today does not mean what it meant in the 1930s; that the percentage of unemployment is much less now than it was then. You can add that today many more married women go out to work. You can stress that, because of the high birthrate in the early 1960s, there is an unusually large number of school leavers this year looking for work and that the same will be true for the next two years. You can emphasise that about a quarter of a million people find new jobs each month and therefore go off the employment register. And you can recall that there are nearly 25 million people in jobs compared with only about 18 million in the 1930s. You can point out that the Labour party conveniently overlooks the fact that of the 2 million unemployed for which they blame us, nearly a million and a half were bequeathed by their government.

But when all that has been said, the fact remains that the level of unemployment in our country today is a human tragedy. Let me make it clear beyond doubt. I am profoundly concerned about unemployment. Human dignity and self-respect are undermined when men and women are condemned to idleness. The waste of a country's most precious assets – the talent and energy of its people – makes it the bounden duty of government to seek a real and lasting cure.

If I could press a button and genuinely solve the unemployment problem, do you think that I would not press that button this instant? Does anyone imagine that there is the smallest political gain in letting this unemployment continue, or that there is some obscure economic religion which demands this unemployment as part of its ritual? This government are pursuing the only policy which gives any hope of bringing our people back to real and lasting employment. It is no coincidence that those countries, of which I spoke earlier, which have had lower rates of inflation have also had lower levels of unemployment.

I know that there is another real worry affecting many of our people. Although they accept that our policies are right, they feel deeply that the burden of carrying them out is falling much more heavily on the private than on the public sector. They say that the public sector is enjoying advantages but the private sector is taking the knocks and at the same time maintaining those in the public sector with better pay and pensions than they enjoy.

I must tell you that I share this concern and understand the resentment. That is why I and my colleagues say that to add to public spending takes away the very money and resources that industry needs to stay in business, let alone to expand. Higher public spending, far from curing unemployment, can be the very vehicle that loses jobs and causes bankruptcies in trade and commerce. That is why we warned local authorities that since rates are frequently the biggest tax that industry now faces, increases in them can cripple local businesses. Councils must, therefore, learn to cut costs in the same way that companies have to.

That is why I stress that if those who work in public

authorities take for themselves large pay increases, they leave less to be spent on equipment and new buildings. That, in turn, deprives the private sector of the orders it needs, especially some of those industries in the hard-pressed regions. Those in the public sector have a duty to those in the private sector not to take out so much in pay that they cause others unemployment. That is why we point out that every time high wage settlements in nationalised monopolies lead to higher charges for telephones, electricity, coal and water, they can drive companies out of business and cost other people their jobs.

If spending money like water was the answer to our country's problems, we would have no problems now. If ever a nation has spent, spent, spent and spent again, ours has. Today that dream is over. All of that money has got us nowhere, but it still has to come from somewhere. Those who urge us to relax the squeeze, to spend yet more money indiscriminately in the belief that it will help the unemployed and the small businessman, are not being kind or compassionate or caring. They are not the friends of the unemployed or the small business. They are asking us to do again the very thing that caused the problems in the first place. We have made this point repeatedly.

I am accused of lecturing or preaching about this. I suppose it is a critic's way of saying, 'Well, we know it is true, but we have to carp at something.' I do not care about that. But I do care about the future of free enterprise, the jobs and exports it provides and the independence it brings to our people. Independence? Yes, but let us be clear what we mean by that. Independence does not mean contracting out of all relationships with others. A nation can be free but it will not stay free for long if it has no friends and no alliances. Above all, it will not stay free if it cannot pay its own way in the world. By the same token, an individual needs to be part of a community and to feel that he is part of it. There is more to this than the chance to earn a living for himself and his family, essential though that is.

Of course, our vision and our aims go far beyond the complex arguments of economics, but unless we get the economy right we shall deny our people the opportunity to share that vision and to see beyond the narrow horizons of economic necessity. Without a healthy economy we cannot have a healthy society. Without a healthy society the economy will not stay healthy for long.

But it is not the state that creates a healthy society. When the state grows too powerful, people feel that they count for less and less. The state drains society, not only of its wealth but of initiative, of energy, the will to improve and innovate as well as to preserve what is best. Our aim is to let people feel that they count for more and more. If we cannot trust the deepest instincts of our people, we should not be in politics at all. Some aspects of our present society really do offend those instincts.

Decent people do want to do a proper job at work, not to be restrained or intimidated from giving value for money. They believe that honesty should be respected, not derided.

They see crime and violence as a threat, not just to society but to their own orderly way of life. They want to be allowed to bring up their children in these beliefs, without the fear that their efforts will be daily frustrated in the name of progress or free expression. Indeed, that is what family life is all about.

There is not a generation gap in a happy and united family. People yearn to be able to rely on some generally accepted standards. Without them you have not got a society at all, you have purposeless anarchy. A healthy society is not created by its institutions, either. Great schools and universities do not make a great nation any more than great armies do. Only a great nation can create and involve great institutions – of learning, of healing, of scientific advance. And a great nation is the voluntary creation of its people – a people composed of men and women whose pride in themselves is founded on the knowledge of what they can give to a community of which they in turn can be proud.

If our people feel that they are part of a great nation and they are prepared to will the means to keep it great, a great nation we shall be, and shall remain. So, what can stop us from achieving this? What then stands in our way? The prospect of another winter of discontent? I suppose it might. But I prefer to believe that certain lessons have been learned from experience, that we are coming, slowly, painfully, to an autumn of understanding. And I hope that it will be followed by a winter of common sense. If it is not, we shall not be diverted from our course.

To those waiting with bated breath for that favourite media catchphrase, the 'U' turn, I have only one thing to say. 'You turn if you want to. The lady's not for turning.' I say that not only to you but to our friends overseas and also to those who are not our friends.

In foreign affairs we have pursued our national interest robustly while remaining alive to the needs and interests of others. Long before we came into office, and therefore long before the invasion of Afghanistan, I was pointing to the threat from the east. I was accused of scaremongering. But events have more than justified my words. Soviet Marxism is ideologically, politically and morally bankrupt. But militarily the Soviet Union is a powerful and growing threat.

Yet it was Mr Kosygin who said, 'No peace loving country, no person of integrity, should remain indifferent when an aggressor holds human life and world opinion in insolent contempt.' We agree. The British government are not indifferent to the occupation of Afghanistan. We shall not allow it to be forgotten. Unless and until the Soviet troops are withdrawn, other nations are bound to wonder which of them may be next. Of course there are those who say that by speaking out we are complicating east-west relations, that we are endangering detente. But the real danger would lie in keeping silent. Detente is indivisible and it is a two-way process.

The Soviet Union cannot conduct wars by proxy in south-east Asia and Africa, foment trouble in the Middle East and Caribbean and invade neighbouring countries and still expect to conduct business as usual. Unless detente is pursued by both sides it can be pursued by neither, and it is a delusion to suppose otherwise. That is the message we shall be delivering loud and clear at the meeting of the European security conference in Madrid in the weeks immediately ahead.

But we shall also be reminding the other parties in Madrid that the Helsinki accord was supposed to promote the freer movement of people and ideas. The Soviet government's response so far has been a campaign of repression worse than any since Stalin's day. It had been hoped that Helsinki would open gates across Europe. In fact, the guards today are better armed and the walls are no lower. But behind those walls the human spirit is unvanquished.

The workers of Poland in their millions have signalled their determination to participate in the shaping of their destiny. We salute them. Marxists claim that the capitalist system is in crisis. But the Polish workers have shown that it is the communist system that is in crisis. The Polish people should be left to work out their own future without external interference.

At every party conference, and every November in parliament, we used to face difficult decisions over Rhodesia and over sanctions. But no longer. Since we last met, the success at Lancaster House, and thereafter in Salisbury – a success won in the face of all the odds – has created new respect for Britain ... We showed over Rhodesia that the hallmarks of Tory policy are, as they have always been, realism and resolve. Not for us the disastrous fantasies of unilateral disarmament, of withdrawal from Nato, of abandoning Northern Ireland.

The irresponsibility of the left on defence increases as the dangers which we face loom larger. We, for our part . . . have chosen a defence policy which potential foes will respect. We are acquiring, with the cooperation of the United States government, the Trident missile system. This will ensure the credibility of our strategic deterrent until the end of the century and beyond, and it was very important for the reputation of Britain abroad that we should keep our independent nuclear deterrent as well as for our citizens here.

We have agreed to the stationing of cruise missiles in this country. The unilateralists object, but the recent willingness of the Soviet government to open a new round of arms control negotiations shows the wisdom of our firmness. We intend to maintain and, where possible, to improve our conventional forces so as to pull our weight in the alliance. We have no wish to seek a free ride at the expense of our allies. We will play our full part.

In Europe we have shown that it is possible to combine a vigorous defence of our own interests with a deep commitment to the idea and to the ideals of the community.

The last government were well aware that Britain's budget contribution was grossly unfair. They failed to do anything about it. We negotiated a satisfactory arrangement which will give us and our partners time to tackle the underlying issues . . . We face many other problems in the community, but I am confident that they too will yield to the firm yet fair approach which has already proved so much more effective than the previous government's five years of procrastination.

With each day it becomes clearer that in the wider world we face darkening horizons, and the war between Iran and Iraq is the latest symptom of a deeper malady. Europe and North America are centres of stability in an increasingly anxious world. The community and the alliance are the guarantee to other countries that democracy and freedom of choice are still possible. They stand for order and the rule of law in an age when disorder and lawlessness are ever more widespread.

The British government intend to stand by both these great institutions, the community and Nato. We will not betray them. The restoration of Britain's place in the world and of the West's confidence in its own destiny are two aspects of the same process. No doubt there will be unexpected twists in the road, but with wisdom and resolution we can reach our goal. I believe we will show the wisdom and you may be certain that we will show the resolution.

In his warm-hearted and generous speech, Peter Thorneycroft said that when people are called upon to lead great nations, they must look into the hearts and minds of the people whom they seek to govern. I would add that those who seek to govern must, in turn, be willing to allow their hearts and minds to lie open to the people.

This afternoon I have tried to set before you some of my most deeply held convictions and beliefs. This party, which

I am privileged to serve, and this government, which I am proud to lead, are engaged in the massive task of restoring confidence and stability to our people.

I have always known that that task was vital. Since last week it has become even more vital than ever. We close our conference in the aftermath of that sinister utopia unveiled at Blackpool. Let Labour's Orwellian nightmare of the Left be the spur for us to dedicate, with a new urgency, our every ounce of energy and moral strength to rebuild the fortunes of this free nation.

If we were to fail, that freedom could be imperilled. So let us resist the blandishments of the faint hearts; let us ignore the howls and threats of the extremists; let us stand together and do our duty, and we shall not fail.

Reproduced with permission from margaretthatcher.org, the official website of the Margaret Thatcher Foundation.

This report of the Conservative party conference ran in the
Guardian on Saturday October 11 1980.

'ORWELLIAN NIGHTMARE' IF TORIES FAIL,
CLAIMS PRIME MINISTER
Thatcher plays on threat of Left to Tory troops

By Ian Aitken, Political Editor

The Prime Minister rattled the grisly bones of last week's
Labour Party Conference at her Conservative faithful yesterday
as the ultimate justification for backing her government.

It was a message addressed beyond the crowded conference hall in Brighton to her vast television audience. With
an angry Right to Work demonstration taking place in the
driving rain outside, it gained a new significance. Delivering
the closing speech of the Conservative Party conference,
accompanied by all the traditional ballyhoo, Mrs Thatcher
spoke of the sinister utopia unveiled at Blackpool and
'Labour's Orwellian nightmare of the Left'.

She told the conference that because of what happened at
Blackpool there was now a heightened awareness that the
Conservative government must succeed. Moments before an
intrepid Left-wing demonstrator who had succeeded in pene-
trating the tight security cordon actually dared to stand up and
shout out some simplistic slogans like 'Power To The Workers'.

Atmosphere of Versailles

He was quickly jumped upon, roughed up a little, and carted out of the hall. The incident served to underline the atmosphere of the Palace of Versailles before the French Revolution which seemed to have entered the souls of some Conservatives in the hall. The conference building was surrounded by a double line of policemen, with the additional precaution of police horses. Amid turmoil and a certain amount of mayhem, some four or five thousand demonstrators were successfully kept away.

But there was real anxiety about a possible breakdown of security as Mrs Thatcher began her speech. Her main message was that the Government was determined to see its policies through to their conclusions.

Determination

To those looking for an imminent U-turn she said: 'You turn if you want to. The lady's not for turning.'

She confessed that there might be an obstacle in the way in the form of another winter of discontent. But she claimed that she preferred to believe that a lesson had been learned from the past, and that the country was coming slowly towards a new Autumn of Understanding, which she hoped would be followed by a Winter of Commonsense.

It has been increasingly obvious this week that ministers are becoming genuinely worried that the Conservative Party is in danger of achieving a damaging identification with economic slump and unemployment. Mrs Thatcher, or perhaps her speechwriters, have clearly taken the message on board.

A substantial passage in her speech dealt with this subject. After a routine attack on the Labour Party, she went on: 'But when all that has been said, the fact remains that the level of unemployment in our country today is a human tragedy. Human dignity and self-respect are undermined when men and women are condemned to idleness.' But if this raised hopes of increased public spending to stimulate new jobs, they were quickly dashed. 'This Government is pursuing the only policy which gives any hope of bringing our people back to real and lasting employment,' she said.

Cabinet critics

She had a few words which might have been directed towards the wets in her own Cabinet. She talked of 'those who urge us to relax the squeeze, to spend yet more money indiscriminately in the belief that it will help the unemployed.' Such people, she said, were not being kind, or compassionate, or caring. They were asking the Government to repeat the very actions which had caused the problems in the first place.

The message was grim, and the mood of the conference this week has been subdued by the problems created by mounting unemployment. But Mrs Thatcher can at least claim to have held the line for another year. She was rewarded with a five and a half minute standing ovation.

The most hunted person
of the modern age

EARL SPENCER
September 6 1997

This speech was delivered at the funeral of Diana,
Princess of Wales, at Westminster Abbey
on September 6 1997.

Beryl Bainbridge

Beryl Bainbridge is a writer. She is working on a
novel about the assassination of Robert Kennedy.

Speeches made at funerals are generally rich in praise for
the departed and full of platitudes. Those unacquainted with
the deceased and the circumstances of death, who are present
simply to give support to one or other members of the
bereaved family, will barely listen to what is said. How
different it was on September 6 1997, when Earl Spencer
delivered the eulogy for his dead sister. Then, the whole
nation, indeed the world, knew of the circumstances
surrounding her passing.

On the Sunday of August 31 1997, some 30 minutes after
midnight, a Mercedes-Benz had driven away from the
Ritz Hotel in Paris pursued by French photographers on
motorcycles. The car, reported to have been travelling at

high speed, entered the Pont de l'Alma tunnel, lost control, swerved sideways on the two-lane carriageway and crashed into the 13th pillar of the underpass. The driver, Henri Paul, and a backseat passenger, Dodi Fayed, were killed instantly. The woman seated next to Fayed was alive but critically injured. Her heart had been displaced from the left to the right side of her chest, tearing the pulmonary vein and the pericardium, causing death some three hours later. She was Diana, Princess of Wales, aged 36.

Prince Charles, staying at Balmoral, was woken at dawn to be told the news. That Sunday he went to church with his boys. The death of Diana was not mentioned in the service, nor were there any prayers relating to it. The minister's sermon contained a joke to do with moving house, followed by a comedy performance given by Billy Connolly. That afternoon the prince flew to Paris to escort the body of his former wife home. Judging by his expression in newsreels, he experienced both sadness and relief. Tony Blair, filmed outside the church earlier in the day, called Diana 'the people's princess'.

And indeed there followed an extraordinary reaction from the public, an upsurge of unprecedented national mourning. The royal family, apparently out of touch with events, remained for a whole week at Balmoral. Newspaper commentaries expressed the country's mood. 'Where is the Queen when the country needs her?' asked the Sun. 'Your people are suffering. Speak to us Ma'am,' wrote another. The Queen returned to London on the eve of the funeral.

Conscious of the public's gathering hostility, Blair must have been relieved when she finally broadcast a tribute to Diana. She was also seen outside Buckingham Palace, apparently on the advice of her staff, patrolling the ramparts of flowers.

The funeral took place in a style both medieval and modern. There was the slow procession from Kensington Palace, single bell mournfully tolling above the clatter of hooves as the horse-drawn carriage bore the coffin to Westminster Abbey; the deafening silence of the vast crowd that lined the route; the solemnity of the church service and the contribution of the singer Elton John who rewrote the words of a song he had originally composed in memory of Marilyn Monroe: 'You called out to our country, and you whispered to those in pain. Now you belong to heaven, and the stars spell out your name. And it seems to me that you lived your life like a candle in the wind.'

And then Earl Spencer got up to speak. At this distance in time and merely produced in print, his eulogy, though heartfelt and full of pain, seems harmless enough. Only when one bears in mind the events surrounding Diana's life – the betrayal shortly after her marriage by the man she loved, her divorce, the removal of her title and the apparent coldness of the royal family towards her – does one begin to see the real meaning behind the words. Spencer stressed that his sister was essentially a British girl, a definition surely aimed at the German background of the royals. She no longer needed, he said, a royal title (earlier removed) to generate her particular brand of magic. Her greatest gift was intuition and a God-given sensitivity towards the sick and underprivileged of the world. He dwelt on her feelings of suffering, her vulnerability, the eating disorder that was a symbol of her insecurity. How different it might have been, he implied, had she been treated with more care by both family and press. He paid tribute to her strength in the face of the most bizarre life imaginable, and spoke of the sadness chewing him up, a description indicating that anger might well choke him. His last sentence thanked God for the happiness Diana had recently known, which was a defiant acknowledgment of her affair with Dodi Fayed.

When he fell silent, the congregation heard a strange sound, that of applause from the crowd outside. They too were showing their pain at the blowing out of their candle in the wind.

The most hunted person of the modern age

EARL SPENCER
September 6 1997

I stand before you today, the representative of a family in grief, in a country in mourning, before a world in shock.

We are all united, not only in our desire to pay our respects to Diana, but rather in our need to do so.

For such was her extraordinary appeal that the tens of millions of people taking part in this service all over the world, via television and radio, who never actually met her, feel that they, too, lost someone close to them in the early hours of Sunday morning. It is a more remarkable tribute to Diana than I can ever hope to offer her today.

Diana was the very essence of compassion, of duty, of style, of beauty. All over the world she was a symbol of self-less humanity, a standard-bearer for the rights of the truly downtrodden, a very British girl who transcended nationality. Someone with a natural nobility who was classless and who proved in the last year that she needed no royal title to continue to generate her particular brand of magic.

Today is our chance to say thank you for the way you brightened our lives, even though God granted you but half a life. We will all feel cheated always that you were taken from us so young, and yet we must learn to be grateful that you came along at all. Only now you are gone do we truly appreciate what we are now without, and we want you to know that life without you is very, very difficult.

We have all despaired at our loss over the past week, and only the strength of the message you gave us through your years of giving has afforded us the strength to move forward.

There is a temptation to rush to canonise your memory. There is no need to do so. You stand tall enough as a human being of unique qualities not to need to be seen as a saint.

Indeed, to sanctify your memory would be to miss out on the very core of your being, your wonderfully mischievous sense of humour, with a laugh that bent you double. Your joy for life transmitted wherever you took your smile and the sparkle in those unforgettable eyes. Your boundless energy, which you could barely contain.

But your greatest gift was your intuition, and it was a gift you used wisely. This is what underpinned all your other wonderful attributes, and if we look to analyse what it was about you that had such a wide appeal, we find it in your instinctive feel for what was really important in all our lives. Without your God-given sensitivity we would be immersed in greater ignorance at the anguish of Aids and HIV sufferers, the plight of the homeless, the isolation of lepers, the random destruction of landmines.

Diana explained to me once that it was her innermost feelings of suffering that made it possible for her to connect with her constituency of the rejected.

And here we come to another truth about her. For all the status, the glamour, the applause, Diana remained throughout a very insecure person at heart, almost childlike in her desire to do good for others so she could release herself from deep feelings of unworthiness, of which her eating disorders were merely a symptom.

The world sensed this part of her character and cherished her for her vulnerability whilst admiring her for her honesty.

The last time I saw Diana was on July 1, her birthday, in London, when typically she was not taking time to celebrate her special day with friends but was guest of honour at a fundraising charity evening. She sparkled of course, but I would rather cherish the days I spent with her in March when she came to visit me and my children in our home in South Africa. I am proud of the fact that, apart from when she was on public display meeting President Mandela, we managed to contrive to stop the ever-present paparazzi from getting a single picture of her – that meant a lot to her.

These were days I will always treasure. It was as if we had been transported back to our childhood when we spent such an enormous amount of time together – the two youngest in the family.

Fundamentally, she had not changed at all from the big sister who mothered me as a baby, fought with me at school and endured those long train journeys between our parents' homes with me at weekends.

It is a tribute to her level-headedness and strength that despite the most bizarre life imaginable after her childhood, she remained intact, true to herself.

There is no doubt that she was looking for a new direction in her life at this time. She talked endlessly of getting away from England, mainly because of the treatment that she received at the hands of the newspapers. I don't think she ever understood why her genuinely good intentions were sneered at by the media, why there appeared to be a permanent quest on their behalf to bring her down. It is baffling.

My own and only explanation is that genuine goodness is threatening to those at the opposite end of the moral spectrum. It is a point to remember that of all the ironies about Diana, perhaps the greatest was this: a girl given the name of the ancient goddess of hunting was, in the end, the most hunted person of the modern age.

She would want us today to pledge ourselves to protecting her beloved boys William and Harry from a similar fate and I do this here, Diana, on your behalf. We will not allow them to suffer the anguish that used regularly to drive you to tearful despair.

And beyond that, on behalf of your mother and sisters, I pledge that we, your blood family, will do all we can to continue the imaginative and loving way in which you were steering these two exceptional young men, so that their souls are not simply immersed by duty and tradition, but can sing openly as you planned.

We fully respect the heritage into which they have both been born, and will always respect and encourage them in their royal role.

But we, like you, recognise the need for them to experience as many different aspects of life as possible to arm them spiritually and emotionally for the years ahead. I know you would have expected nothing less from us.

William and Harry, we all care desperately for you today. We are all chewed up with sadness at the loss of a woman who was not even our mother. How great your suffering is we cannot even imagine.

I would like to end by thanking God for the small mercies he has shown us at this dreadful time, for taking Diana at her most beautiful and radiant and when she had joy in her private life.

Above all, we give thanks for the life of a woman I am so proud to be able to call my sister: the unique, the complex, the extraordinary and irreplaceable Diana, whose beauty, both internal and external, will never be extinguished from our minds.

Speech copyright © The Earl Spencer.

The following reports ran in the *Guardian* on Monday,
September 8 1997. They have been abridged.

THE FUNERAL OF DIANA

Brother's rapier thrust that left the Windsors wounded

By Kamal Ahmed, Luke Harding and Sarah Boseley

The voice only started cracking towards the end, as emotion
started to overtake the bite of the content. But already the
rapier wound had been inflicted. Five minutes that shook
the royal world. They will be returned to again and again.
That oration at that funeral. The words that caused the winds
of applause already swirling around the crowds outside to
overwhelm the congregation, rushing from the back of
Westminster Abbey to the front, catching finally the royal
family itself.

William clapped. Harry clapped. Prince Charles tapped
his thigh and then immediately stopped. The Queen, Prince
Philip and the Queen Mother did not move. Maybe the
words had already penetrated their minds. The bitterness of
the attack, the references to 'blood family', to the dangers
of duty, to the princess's bizarre royal life that had left the
stains of anguish and tearful despair.

When the talk is of monarchy, as it inevitably will be
over the next weeks, those 1,200 words will be the mark

of whether the royal family has progressed towards an open, more popular future or fallen back on the stiffness of tradition and silence. Lord St John of Fawsley said yesterday that the monarchy can only continue if supported by public opinion. Earl Spencer has fired the first shot across the bows.

Blood family

'On behalf of your mother and sisters, I pledge that we, your blood family, will do all we can to continue the imaginative and loving way in which you were steering these two exceptional young men, so that their souls are not simply immersed by duty and tradition, but can sing openly as you planned.'

One word cut, a sharp edge of a razor blade. Blood. A word heavy with the imagery of honour and family line. A word at the very foundation of the monarchy. A word which will forever divide Diana from Charles and the Queen.

Yesterday, as those in the prince's camp were trying to collect their thoughts after such an attack, there were already the rumblings of anger. What right does this man have to lecture Prince Charles? What credentials, if any, do the Spencers have to claim the happy families high ground? Friends of Prince Charles also point out that the use of the word 'duty', as if some form of insult, reveals a lack of understanding of the position William and Harry find themselves in.

'I don't think she ever understood why her genuinely good intentions were being sneered at by the media.'

And so from the royal family to the media. Many expected

the tribute spoken to a hushed abbey to contain some reference to the newspapers Earl Spencer had accused of having 'blood on their hands' the day after his sister's death. He did not disappoint. The earl wants something to be done, and his plea struck a resonant chord with the public. Mr Blair has said it is time for considered action.

'Diana was the very essence of compassion, of duty, of style, of beauty. Someone with a natural nobility who was classless and who proved in the last year that she needed no royal title to continue to generate her particular brand of magic.'

On the surface, much of the tribute is in straightforward praise of the princess. But the words referring to Diana's 'nobility' and the mention of 'no royal title' were in fact a sharp attack to those who remember the final, fractious argument between Diana and the royal family before the divorce. There were calls last week for the title Her Royal Highness to be reinstated posthumously to the princess. Again, Earl Spencer was tapping into a rich vein of public support.

She may be at peace. The nation is not
By Matthew Engel

Now we begin to understand why the most popular and enduring tragic plays of history have been written about kings and princes and earls, and not about, say, the European Union or the Parliamentary Labour Party. This was probably the most public occasion the world has ever known. Earl Spencer used it to come as near as anyone has done within Britain since 1745 to raising the rebel standard against the monarchy. His address was not a eulogy, but a battle cry.

Even before he began, one observer in Westminster Abbey thought the scene resembled the House of Commons. The Spencers in the North Lantern staring across at the Windsors in the South Lantern, a couple of sword-lengths away. But these are two families that match each other, and any political party, for internal dysfunction, for the range of their splits, feuds, sub-feuds, and even the odd lingering cross-current of affection. Now they are ranged, institutionally, against each other: Montagues and Capulets for our times, but with the war outlasting both love and death.

Tragedy of Charles III

The life of Diana was a tragic story. We may now be embarking on the sequel: The Tragedy of Charles III. But maybe there is never going to be a Charles III.

And if there is, then in the overblown atmosphere of this weekend one could be forgiven for wondering whether it really will be Charles Windsor rather than Charles Spencer, the new popular hero, and a far more gifted moment-seizer than the Windsors have ever produced.

After all, how will he respond if the royals dig in and he does not get his way on the boys' future upbringing? He is godson to the Queen, ex-brother-in-law to the Prince of Wales and uncle to Prince William, the perfect CV for a vengeful medieval usurper.

In the Mall, as the crowd began to drift away, the support

for Earl Spencer seemed unanimous. 'Fantastic,' said an elderly gent from Chester, who had just camped out for the first time in his life. 'Right on the button,' said a man from Hounslow. 'I thought he was excellent,' said a middle-aged lady from Luton. But hadn't he sort of declared war on the royal family? 'Oh, yes,' she replied, 'just a touch.'

It was the strangest imaginable climax to this strange and mournful day. Despite the vast throng in the Mall and Whitehall, there was a silence the streets of central London never hear these days, not even at five in the morning.

There were no clouds in the sky. The sun glinted on the St James's Park lake, and the stonework of the palace gleamed. It felt like the capital of a different, distant country.

When the ceremony began, the royals froze into their characteristic poses: the Queen sphinx-like, the Prince of Wales as if broken, William masking his feelings with what looked like boredom. Tony Blair taking his control of the significant pause close to the point of self-parody. Then Elton John, professionalism carrying him through when everyone insisted he would break down.

Sound of distant rain

It was at this moment that we heard the sound which several writers have compared to distant rain. That is precisely what it was like. It was the crowd in Parliament Square applauding. Inside there was one applaud, hastily stopped. No one claps at funerals. Not in England. Or rather, no one used to clap at funerals.

Then came Earl Spencer. Let's be cool about this. His address contained elements of disingenuousness bordering on mendacity. To describe Diana v the tabloids as an encounter between 'genuine goodness' and total evil is a grotesque distortion of a complex relationship. When he warned against sanctifying her memory, he said that was wrong, but only because of her 'mischievous sense of humour'. Even in a funeral oration, it is customary to paint over the cracks more convincingly than that.

The urge for vengeance was one of Diana's characteristics, and it runs in the family. This was a brilliantly crafted oration. Maybe he is the master phrasemaker, maybe he had help. But in his amazing climax, he used words and phrases – 'blood family', 'sing openly' – whose force he understood perfectly.

Like his dead sister, and unlike the Windsors, he knows the power of word, and gesture, and symbol. He despises those who convey the symbols to the masses. He has not resolved the paradox.

Then came the rain again. And this time it spread inside. It would be fascinating to work out exactly who did and did not applaud, who did so wilfully, who half-heartedly and who because they simply forgot themselves and followed the herd. William and Harry clapped, Charles was seen to tap his thigh, Hyde Park erupted.

The most beautiful moment of all, for me, was the choir of angels singing her to her rest with the hymn to the tune of *Danny Boy*. But this was no longer a funeral any more, not even this most fervid of funerals. It had gone way beyond that. The body of a beautiful, gifted, kind, flawed, fated human being lies on the island at Althorp. A huge proportion of the population believes she is Diana, saint and martyr, victim of the wicked Windsors. She may be at peace. The nation is not.